Following a varied career as naval engineer, political journalist, novelist and publisher, Sylvester Stein, at the age of 51, took up running in 1972. He went on to become a British and European champion sprinter and was the World champion veteran runner for the 200m. Today, he still competes nationally and internationally and is, in addition, Chairman of the British Veterans Athletic Federation. He is also founder-publisher of *Running Magazine*. He lives in London and enjoys reading, art, theatre and, of course, running. He is Britain's fastest old-age pensioner!

99

WAYS TO REACH

100

Step-by-Step Advice
for a Long, Healthy, Happy Life

SYLVESTER STEIN

CENTURY
LONDON · MELBOURNE · AUCKLAND · JOHANNESBURG

Copyright © Sylvester Stein 1987

First published in 1987 by
Century Hutchinson Ltd,
Brookmount House, 62–65 Chandos Place,
Covent Garden, London WC2N 4NW

Century Hutchinson Australia Pty Ltd
PO Box 496,
16–22 Church Street,
Hawthorn, Victoria 3122
Australia

Century Hutchinson New Zealand Limited
PO Box 40–086,
Glenfield, Auckland 10
New Zealand

Century Hutchinson South Africa Pty Ltd
PO Box 337,
Bergvlei 2012,
South Africa

Filmset in Linotron Baskerville by
Deltatype Ltd, Ellesmere Port, Cheshire

Printed and bound in Great Britain by
Richard Clay Ltd, Bungay, Suffolk

British Library Cataloguing in Publication Data

Stein, Sylvester
    99 ways to reach 100 : step-by-step
    advice for a long, healthy, happy life.
    1. Health
    I. Title
    613   RA776

ISBN 0–7126–1648–9

CONTENTS

If I'd known I was going to live this long,
I'd have taken more care of myself.

Pianist Eubie Blake
on his 100th birthday

Your first hundred years: A Preface

In the twentieth century Man has discovered how to prolong the life of the species and has learned to exercise greater concern for the life of the individual. Mega deaths, by war and famine, though still fearful enough, have decreased; at the same time the death-rates of ordinary human beings from infant mortality, infectious disease and such self-induced causes as smoking and the motor car have continued downwards. We are living longer.

While the scientists and the agencies of care continue to devote themselves to that cause of long life, they are in addition working on ways to stay the ageing process. In these last few years medical research has begun to make some significant advances; by the time the twenty-first century arrives, we will be living longer younger.

This book is a guide to preserving yourself for that time. It tells how in the meanwhile you can avoid needless exposure to the major killing factors as well as sidestep the minor ones, sudden or slow; and it lists the main ways open to promoting spirited and enjoyable life.

There are schemes and safeguards for those already past their prime to keep them going vigorously until their century and even beyond – stay alive to 125!

For those who are young today the message is: take good care of yourself, you may live for ever. After all, there is no implicit reason why animals should die off at all, let alone decline from their prime. Science and civilization are speeding up efforts to conquer the ageing process and to improve and increase the replacement of worn body parts. Before long there will be universal warehouses of regenerated and man-made hearts, kidneys, lungs, arteries, limbs . . . even brains.

Centenarians will soon become the norm and will be as strong and vigorous as the young. Then 150 years of age will become common. By the new century we will be able to outlast the redwoods. . . . We will have it in our grasp to live for ever.

It will happen because it's the way evolution will move in its requirement to economize on human material. Why waste the world's assets in people? It is more efficient to keep them going on and on than to start from scratch, developing and educating the young. Why throw away human vessels with their precious cargoes of knowledge and experience? Why allow them to decline and die?

If you want to join the destiny ship and sail in it for ever, now is the time to act.

WAYS

1~10

FITNESS AND EXERCISE

The biggest killers in our society are heart disease and cancer. In a sense all death is defined by heart failure. It follows that strengthening the heart is the best way of lengthening life. The heart is the most important muscle in the body, and it supplies all tissues with essential oxygen and nutrients. Like the motor of a car, it is the primary active force.

For cardiac health the major factor, along with controlling fat intake and stress, is exercise, the surest guarantee of longevity.

The famously long-lived people of the Caucasus are peasant farmers. They work in the fields, active and fit until 100. The Hunzas of Pakistan have a similar hard-working lifestyle and are renowned for sprightliness in old age. Shegichiyo Izumi of Japan, who died in February 1986, ascribed his vitality to hard work in the fields and a frugal diet. He was the only person known with certainty to have reached 120. Indeed, the Japanese now have the longest life expectancy of any people in the world, probably as a result of their much lower rate of heart disease.

Of course, for most of us farm work is not possible. So we have to replace it with other forms of exercise, which simulate the natural work the human body needs. In the following pages, I suggest ten most effective contributions to getting fit. There are of course many other ways, from mud wrestling to kangaroo boxing, all of them with their particular benefits and drawbacks. The important thing is regularity; half an hour a day, even just two hours a week, will get priceless oxygen into the system and strengthen the all-important heart.

Even for the delicate, exercise can add years of happy life. The novelist Somerset Maugham is a good case in point. He was always constitutionally a bit below par, at one stage confined to a sanatorium with tuberculosis. However, through a programme of regular daily swimming in his later years, plus dietary moderation, he passed 90. *Four score years and ten – that's your minimum for today.*

1

ABOVE ALL, RUNNING!
Surest, safest, cheapest, best way to fitness

If ever you see a herd of club runners galloping through the park of a Sunday there's one thing you'll note they have in common: the men and women, the pre-teens and the veterans, every one of them will look really fit. For running is the exercise that does most for the heart and the lungs – that's what provides the reality and the appearance of fitness. Running is also the surest, safest, and cheapest exercise system and it's the most natural, the most effective, and the most pleasant. No wonder people in other sports take up jogging for *their* fitness.

Since Dr Kenneth Cooper discovered the remarkable facts of how running strengthens the heart, it became America's, then the world's Number One form of exercise, the Number One method of avoiding heart disease, mankind's biggest killer. Today there are 300 million joggers, in the USA, Britain, Africa, France, South America, Japan . . . and wherever there's a road.

Whatever your state of fitness you can start out running now. No need to consult your doctor unless you already are a heart case. Even then running, under supervision, is often good treatment. Whatever your age you can take it up without worry, but heed advice on pace and technique to avoid the common problems of backache and hip complaints. Arley Nicholls of Melbourne, Australia, had watched her husband Stan running all their married life. Stan was an Olympic athlete before the

---

RUN FUN

★ Jenny Wood Allen, a town councillor of Dundee, Scotland, aged 71, successfully completed her first marathon on only six weeks training.

★ In Rome, June 1985, three men over 90 years of age contested the 100m sprint at world championship level. Azad Pirthi Singh of India won the gold.

★ Dr Kenneth Cooper of Dallas, Texas, has more than 200 heart patients training for the marathon.

★ In the 1986 London marathon 5020 of the entrants had never run a marathon before.

★ An over-60-years American ran the 100m race faster in 1986 than the Olympic champion of 1896.

Getting out and doing it

Here are some devices to get you out running the first time if you're too self-conscious – or lazy. After the first few runs it becomes catching.

1 Buy yourself a superb pair of training shoes . . . you'll *have* to try them out.
2 Pull a balaclava over your head; the neighbours won't recognize you.
3 Get sponsored by your favourite charity for the local fun run . . . you'll not want to let them down.
4 Take a dog for a trot in the park; he'll pull you along . . .
5 . . . so will a couple of kids.
6 Wrap up in extra layers of clothing, then you don't need to use the weather as an excuse.

Then, a few basic rules for beginners:
1 Little and often – a regular 12 minutes five times a week.
2 Why go on your own? Team up with a couple of other new-breed runners for company and for encouragement.
3 Train, don't Strain – give your body a chance, don't become too obsessive about your running once you're into it.

war and still running at 75 in the veteran section – as tough and fit as old boots. Arley at 70 finally bought herself a pair of road trainers and took on the champion in the family. She built up a solid number of slow miles in training, entered a couple of veteran races and finally had the pleasure of beating Stan in a handicap event.

Of course running need not be competitive; that merely makes it extra fun. According to physiologists, all you need to give your heart complete protection is to jog a slow 20 minutes three or four times a week. A small price to pay for a possible extra decade of good healthy life!

In addition to the heart-and-lungs benefits, running will improve your body tone, your mobility, your mental alertness, your confidence and your co-ordination.

How to take it up then and how to keep it up? Don some comfortable clothes and plimsolls and jog straight out through the gate. For your first runs adopt the classic lamp-post to lamp-post training scheme for beginners: jog very slowly, barely lifting your feet, to the first post, then *walk* towards the next; then jog, then walk – for some ten minutes in all. Go out three times a week, urging yourself slightly further each time and convert one of the walks into a jog. Before long you're a runner!

AEROBICS
Blood will flow!

No need to be a dancer to go gathering aerobics. The word aerobic, meaning 'living on oxygen from the air', was coined to describe those helpful bacteria inside compost heaps that take in air to breathe. Now it's used for the kind of exercise that obliges you to keep breathing air in deeply, sending oxygen swirling round your bloodstream. Thus it was re-coined by Dr Cooper in his book *Aerobics*, which showed that continuous deep-breathing builds up the muscle of your heart, which then survives longer. And so do you.

In fact, strengthening the heart like that through sessions of sustained activity is probably the single most important positive thing you can do to prolong healthy life. It's at the top of the 99 Ways. It's more effective than diet, more beneficial than tablets, more valuable to you than all the money in the world.

And it's easier than falling off a log. That's why aerobic dancing became popular, because everyone found it easy and fun, a great way to get in the amount of continuous exercising movements that are needed. Other good ways are jogging, swimming, cycling, walking, gardening; calling for endurance efforts rather than the now-and-then explosive actions of sprinting, jumping and throwing. Those fast and explosive athletes make use of oxygen already in their system; there you have anaerobics, the word for the type of bug buried deeper down in the compost that doesn't use air for its supply of oxygen.

AEROBIOLOGICALITIES

★ The heart pumps 5 litres of blood a minute at rest; 25 litres a minute during a hard run.

★ The heart rate of a racing canoeist goes to 195 beats a minute.

★ Through training a person can increase his blood volume by half a litre. And the blood circulates more easily.

★ Through training the number of fine capillary blood vessels will increase by 20 per cent, and the amount of the muscle oxygen transporting substance, myoglobin, will increase 50 per cent.

★ The increased oxygen flow gives an extra sense of well-being and mood enhancement.

Test how speedily you get fit

Here's an easy, interesting and dramatic way to note your improving fitness when you take up an aerobic exercise.

Write down your pulse rate when you first decide to go in for jogging, swimming, aerobic dance or whatever. Take the pulse in the morning, when still lying in bed. This is to give you a constant reference. It may be in the 70s or 80s, which is considered 'normal', though it's really only normal for sedentary people.

Then take it again each week. Keep a table or graph. It should drop downwards steadily after only a few weeks, and will stay down all your life as long as you keep in touch with aerobics. You can expect a reading in the 50s or 60s. If you turn into a dedicated marathoner or swimmer, it will be in the 40s. There are some ultra-distance runners who tick over at 36 or 38! All this is a sign of a good, healthy heart. The sedentary person's heartbeat simply *flutters*.

The most surprising of Cooper's findings, since confirmed by other exercise scientists, is that you don't need to exercise very hard or very long to get full health value for your heart. So, no excuses, absolutely anyone is capable of going in for it. If it's jogging, you need only 20-minute sessions of slow running three or four times a week. Depending on how hard you stride out, 35-minute walks would do it. These are absolutely not *athletic* endeavours. What counts when you're doing it for health is the continuousness – you must keep going with barely a stop or a slow-down.

That's sensational, really, quite magical. It is worth repeating, if only to persuade the faint-hearted. Not to mention that it will make them strong-hearted!

To provide invaluable protection for your heart all you need each week is a few continuous 20-minute sessions of very moderate exercise.

Cooper has provided sets of simple tables showing the points to be earned from various exercises. The best value of a points system such as this is that it gives you an incentive and a target. Then you don't just sit back and do nothing . . . lest suddenly you find: That was the Week that Was, and where were you? Sedentary all seven days!

Add up all the advantages: offers you a strong heart, reduces your chances of coronaries, makes you feel good in mind and body, helps you relax, assists you to stay slim, gets you more supple . . . it's enjoyable, and it costs practically nothing.

CYCLING
Free-wheeling to fitness

Cycling stands high on the list of activities that are both good for you and bad for you. It is among the finest aerobic exercises of all, benefiting the whole range of users from elite athlete to vicar's wife, and yet it treats many of its followers abominably, injuring 30,000 cyclists a year on the road and causing the deaths of 300.

Cycling is mainly an endurance activity. Even what racing cyclists term sprinting is quite a long-winded effort compared to the runner's 60m or 100m dash. It is endurance training that produces the aerobic essentials, increasing the size of the heart and improving the efficiency of the heart, lung and blood systems.

Because of the way it picks up a sportsman's aerobic fitness cycling often produces fine distance *runners* too. Les Pendlebury, top cyclist, immediately became a top cross-country runner when switching from the one sport to the other . . . so did Laurie Forster . . . so did Jack Foster, world marathon ace, and many another.

Its endurance characteristic also makes cycling a great fitness appliance for strict amateurs, such as the vicar's wife, who not only uses it for her shopping trips but also plans, these fitness-conscious days, to get body trimming thrown in.

CYCLING NUMBERS

★ The lungs at rest process 10 litres of air per minute; a racing cyclist in action processes 200. Cyclists are among the sportsmen with the largest hearts.

★ Distance cycling is the sport in which women's performance comes closest to men's.

★ A new bicycle can be bought for as little as £79 – or as much as £800.

★ The first road death of a pedal cyclist was in 1870.

★ By 1907 the rate had risen to 253.

★ There are four male to one female cycling fatalities per annum.

★ The death risk of cycling is ten times that of travelling by car, but only half of that by motor bike.

The extreme is finally reached when the get-you-there function of the cycle is rejected altogether and a stationary machine is installed in the living room solely for fitness's sake.

As well as this cardiovascular fitness, cycling provides other valuable attributes for sportsman and health seeker: extra muscle strength and flexibility.

Cycling as a sport covers a wide range of activities. There are track and road, with time trialling, also cyclo-cross, and now there is the triathlon, where cycling has emerged as one of the key three sports that make it up – running and swimming being the others.

Cycling as a way of fitness can claim to feed the hand that bites it: it has become the fashion for men and women during the 1980s to get their exercise in by cycling to work – and are they not well repaid by the savings on commuter transport? This soon covers the capital cost of the machine.

The next stage is to join a local club and soon you will be beguiled into going on one of the long country runs or into joining in the mass London to Brighton ride. From this you can expect an extra measure of fitness beyond the basic heart and lung protection from the daily ride to work.

The stage after that is full-scale racing. You move up from membership of the Cyclists Touring Club to the British Cycling Federation and finally you hope to don the yellow jersey of the Milk Race leader.

Race cycling, as ordinary push-biking, has a special appeal for those in their thirties and forties. There is a flourishing veterans' cycling group, both women and men going in for competition over distances up to 100 miles. They ride tandems, tricycles, even tandem-trikes, not only the humble two-wheeler.

What about the bad news? Although the numbers of cycling casualties is slowly decreasing there are still far too many – the fault of the road authorities, the careless motorists and casual cyclists themselves. Too many still take chances. Some even ignore drink warnings . . . 15 cyclists killed on the roads in 1984 were over the legal limit. Finally the carelessness of some cyclists caused 800 accidents involving pedestrians!

An important point is to take particular care at T-junctions. A government study has shown that many cycle accidents occur there . . . in one-third of them motorists turned across the path of the cyclist who was going straight on.

Another danger: culverts and grooves. They tip you right over on to your thigh. A friend who has come through wars, survived biking tours through the wild, expeditions up Everest and high-flying junkets everywhere finally succumbed to a suburban tramline in Amsterdam and needed a steel pin in the top of his femur. He was lucky to avoid a metal joint replacement and was thus eventually able to continue his adventurous life.

DANCE
Enjoy yourself, it's good for you

In remotest times dancing was a communal art – and a comprehensive one: it took in magic and therapy as well as a goodly measure of entertainment. While the masses were enjoying the entertainment the tribal magician was conjuring up spirits to help with his smelling out and healing.

The role of the dance hasn't changed that much. Entertainment is there today in plenty, we expect pure magic in the staging of the shows – and nobody lacks for therapeutic exercise. Perhaps the arrangements are less communal today, the dancers, elevated beyond the reach of the tribe, being the only ones to get their exercise then and there. The rest of us have to go in search of it.

Where? You can find it in aerobic groups, in ballet, mime and movement classes and even in ballroom dancing of all kinds, though you have to be sure of getting down to it two or three times a week for full fitness benefit.

The ballet dancer of course gets down to it every day of the week and for three or four hours at a time. The warm-up routines alone can occupy professional dancers more than an

---

DANCING FIGURES

★ The feet contain 52 bones, a quarter of the total number in the body.

★ In classical ballet the arms are considered the most expressive parts of the body. Maya Plisetskaya, of the Bolshoi, a renowned dancer and teacher, once said: 'The arms are everything.'

★ Louis XIV, the Sun King, earned his nickname from early appearances in court ballets. He performed from the age of thirteen, and took daily lessons for much of his life.

★ Spanish flamenco has its origins not in Spain but in India.

★ Nijinsky is reputed to be the only person ever to have executed an 'entrechat-dix'.

★ There are animals that execute formal dances, in every major group: fish, insects, reptiles, birds and mammals.

Dancing do's and dancing don't's

1 Warm up thoroughly before starting your movements. You'll need a longer warm-up if you're older – at least 15 mins – until the body is fully stretched and perspiration shows.

2 Cool down and relax gradually after a session. A modest tot of whisky or brandy can help.

3 Make sure you find a sympathetic teacher. A good teacher will protect you from needless injury.

4 Never neglect good nutrition. Anorexia is too common among serious dancers, and you need to keep up stamina and general health.

hour – limbering and stretching movements simply to enable them to tackle the work-outs proper. At the end of a day's training, they are fit, very fit. Then there might be a performance in the evening. Some dancers do weight training sessions as well and claim to be as fit as any sportsman.

These are some of the ways that dancing can be used to improve health and vigour. For a start, as it did long ago, it helps the participants to integrate themselves socially, no better a way of assisting mental well-being. It keeps the brain alert too, through bringing concentration to bear on self-coordination.

It strengthens the body and makes it more supple as well as providing vital cardiovascular training. Suppleness insures you against injury to muscles and bone whereas the training for the heart supplies stamina, worth years of extra life.

Often enough dance is used as a direct form of therapy, to treat conditions such as anxiety, uncontrollable aggression and depression. Dance classes are appreciated for the way they improve the pupils' ability to concentrate – backward children are observed to become more interested in their studies.

Dance classes are usually cheap and easy to join. There are scores of types to choose from. A short selection:

Ballet: mostly for the young, but some adult classes
Contemporary: less stylized than ballet, more fun
Jazz: induces strong rhythmic coordination
Stage: includes tap, modern dance, ballet
Kathak: Indian dance, most graceful
Morris dancing: mostly for men
Irish dancing: the feet do most of the work here
Plus: body popping, break-dancing, disco, rock 'n' roll, jitterbugging, clog dancing, belly dancing, Scottish dancing, Spanish flamenco, kwela and a hundred other national styles.

5 PUMPING IRON
Fitness by the hundredweight

Total end-to-end fitness from a weight-training regime brings you little extra lifespan beyond what you earn with moderate exercise. Nevertheless it has hidden advantages. Not only do you get that sparkling fitness feeling all over, in every single little tingle of your muscles, but being more deeply involved in its pursuit like this helps you to stay with it. There's less danger of becoming a back-slider.

That's especially so if you join a class. It offers fixed times and group routines to keep you at it. With no outside discipline how easy it is to slump back into an amiable programme of four square meals a day and no work-out.

The range of weight-training options is extreme. Once there were only free weights – barbells and dumb-bells – but now there is every sort of stand-alone or multi-structured machine, as well as soft and fluffy variations of the original iron weights. Though nothing is quite like that real stuff . . . where clever exercises can get at each and every muscle in the body, in the end more precisely even than a circuit of 40 Nautilus units. It must be said, however, that loose weights can be dangerous in the hands of an uninstructed beginner.

Start modestly and build up. First try out that old standard, the stationary bicycle. Often its fate is to be left unused and abandoned, so make a resolution to climb on it every single day. If you stick to it, there is much to be gained, both in overall aerobic fitness and specific muscle toning. Interval training –

TRUTHS AND UNTRUTHS

★ True: the use of weights in training adds strength without bulk.

★ Untrue: weightlifters' bodies are inflexible.

★ Untrue: when you give up weight training your muscle turns to fat.

★ True: work with weights improves a woman's figure.

★ True: weights work is an excellent substitute programme for an injured athlete.

★ True: you need to spend as much time on the warm-up and stretching session as on the actual weights work-out!

What weights?

The key to weight training is choosing the proper weight, whether you're using free weights or multi-gym equipment. Of course, the right weight differs from person to person. But there's an easy rule. The proper weight for an exercise is the one with which you can do 12 to 15 repetitions – the last repetition of each set of a particular exercise being hard, very hard. The reason: to develop strength the muscle must try to do more work than it is used to. That is what training means.

As you progress it will require a heavier weight to get you to that same 'just-about' point. That is the benefit of training!

Over two or three sessions you will develop the programme that suits your own needs. Make notes, so that you don't have the bother all over again each time. And remember you're not going in for single big heaves like the weight-lifters; think always in terms of repetitions.

that is, speeded-up stretches sandwiched between slow recovery stretches – is a good session for a bike; it takes the boredom out of watching the minutes go past, as well.

Alternative basics are treadmills, rebound joggers or rowing machines – all better than bullworker-type apparatus, which doesn't get the whole body working.

Now, with some understanding of the subject, you could look for your ideal weights equipment. A small set of free weights catering for yourself only, plus a training bench, is going to be one of the cheapest systems, but today there are also, and not too unreasonably priced, compact machines with their own weight stacks for a home gym. Some of these, though elementary, are very versatile, to handle a variety of upper body and leg exercises.

For runners there are new inventions, soft and comfortable, of strap-on weights to go jogging with, in a bid to improve overall strength and flexibility.

For the deep thinker: the backswing, a machine to hang you upside down, or on an incline, so that the spine is stretched out –and the blood is sent to the head. This enriches the supply of nutrients to the brain, improving memory and concentration!

The right mixture, the backswinger and a jogging machine, perhaps, catering for head and toe, will offer as nice a set of extremes as you might desire. When it's your life you're providing for, there's no need to be too moderate about it.

T'AI CHI
No safer way to fitness

T'ai chi draws inspiration from the Chinese philosophies of Taoism and Confucianism, and places great importance on prevention as being the best cure. It's a unique set of exercises designed to improve the circulation of the blood, promote deep and relaxed breathing, and prevent illness.

It has the advantage of being open to everyone, with the exception of young children. There is no upper age restriction, and it can be done by all, whether strong, weak, male, female, old, young, or pregnant.

T'ai chi is not strenuous exercise and is thus probably one of the safest ways to keep fit. The emphasis is on slow, relaxed movements, with no strain on the muscles. The heart is not over-activated, and energy is conserved. No chance of injury.

The art of t'ai chi is connected with the martial arts, though originally t'ai chi was not associated with aggression but rather with spirituality.

THE T'AI CHI MOVEMENT

★ T'ai chi originally meant 'ridgepole', central support or mainstay – the link that bridges Heaven and Earth. Later it came to mean 'supreme ultimate'.

★ T'ai chi is based on the principle that humans are made for *movement*. The discipline involves continuous, though relaxed, movement.

★ T'ai chi originated in China in the eleventh century. Its present form is younger – dating from the fourteenth century.

★ One of the legendary founders of t'ai chi was a monk who was concerned about the damaging effects of a sedentary lifestyle.

★ Chinese sages originally developed their health philosophy in an attempt to live for ever. The experiment failed, so they settled for second best: a good, long life.

★ In t'ai chi the free passage of energy through and out of the body eliminates staleness and replenishes one with incoming life-force. This particularly occurs through the hands and feet, which develop sensitivity and healing ability.

The English equivalent of the word 'chi' is probably the phrase 'intrinsic energy'. The beginner should commence by relaxing completely and aim to throw every bone and muscle of the body wide open so that the 'chi' can travel freely. Next, the chest is further relaxed and the 'chi' made to sink to the navel. Later the student will learn to accumulate the energy, which can then be directed with his mind to any part of the body.

It is essential to learn with a good teacher. There are often classes held at dance studios.

There are 37 postures, with repetitions added, which, depending on the school being taught, can be extended to 60 or 150 postures. Each posture has its name. Posture 1 is 'Preparation'. The student stands erect, facing north, feet pointed ahead, shoulder width apart, knees bent slightly. Elbows are down. Posture 2 is 'Beginning'. Inhale slowly, raise arms upward to shoulder height. Wrists should be bent, fingers hanging down, with arms at shoulder height, and with fingers extended. Then the arms are drawn back by bending the elbows. Try these postures slowly and carefully.

Many have poetic titles – like Posture 3, 'Grasp sparrow's tail', in which the movement of slowly rolling a large ball is simulated. Other names include 'Stork spreads wings', 'Step back and repulse monkey', 'Diagonal flying', 'Fair lady works at shuttles', 'Step forward to seven stars', 'Bend bow and shoot tiger'.

All movements should be performed with a calm but concentrated mind, and a relaxed body. One should aim to walk like a cat (light and firm), and move as though swimming in air.

They are all continuous movement patterns, perfectly exact and choreographed. There are no static positions, as each movement flows gradually into the next, performed at the same pace.

Daily practice is stressed to reap the full benefits. But as a cycle only lasts 10–15 minutes, it's not too demanding. The Chinese practise at dawn and dusk. You may have seen pictures on TV of sometimes quite elderly men and women performing t'ai chi in their blue work overalls. You don't need much space (four feet on one side), and you can practise with friends or alone. You'll be rewarded with a healthy body, an increasingly alert mind and a feeling of tranquillity.

If you can't find a teacher, there are illustrated books available at shops and libraries.

In the same gentle tradition as t'ai chi, the Chinese are now going in for Qigong, a 'low energy consumption' exercise. Qigong is a system of breathing exercises performed in a sitting or lying position. Oxygen intake falls and the metabolism rate decreases, leaving more resources for fighting disease. Said to cure blood pressure, angina and partial paralysis.

FOOTWORK
Walkways to health

Walking to work is the new superstar of the fitness show, recently rated top of the bill by science. It's a modest little exercise, previously thought of as no more than a walk-on. Yet now it's been promoted to this important role in the do-it-yourself longevity act. That's come about through a research study on the lives and deaths of 15,000 Harvard men after leaving college.

Dr Ralph S. Paffenbarger Jr measured the health of the Harvard old boys over two decades and discovered that those who had exercised regularly gained years of extra health and life. His experiments, long and thorough, were the first the medical profession would accept as proof of the point, although not so surprising to the rest of us.

But here's the big new point: the exercises that were found effective did not have to be excessively vigorous; in fact activities such as walking city blocks and stair-climbing got top marks.

That is all excellent news for those who cannot, for whatever reason, manage the high-velocity business of running. And that

---

MORE THAN ONE STEP FOR MANKIND

★ In the USA there are 55 million exercise walkers.

★ The average Briton walks 100,000 miles in a lifetime.

★ Major weekend pursuit in Germany is the Volkslauf, a walk event for the whole family.

★ Friedrich Nietzsche: 'A sedentary life is the real sin against the Holy Spirit. Only those thoughts that come by walking have value.'

★ The Los Niños Marathon is a 250-mile walk race in California.

★ Hard walking burns more calories than light jogging.

★ There are some 100 models of special trekking or walking shoes now on the market.

★ It took Ned Gillette four months to walk around the base of Mt Everest.

A programme for exercise walking

1 The check-up. Make certain shoes and socks are in perfect shape, don comfortable clothes.
2 The warm-up. Do about ten minutes of light physical activity, to get the breathing going and the pulse rate up.
3 The stretching routine. Slowly stretch out your calves and thigh muscles, windmill your arms.
4 The work-out. If you're new at it or unfit, do a 30-minute non-stop walk (3 times a week) at 3 mph. If physically in shape make it 4 to 5 mph.
5 The warm-down. Take a few minutes to cool down: a slow stroll and more stretching.

news has spread fast; we can already observe worldwide the beginnings of a walking boom. Now you can foresee the next rush-hour fashion, commuters crowding the pavements, rather like joggers in Central Park or cyclists in Holland, the faster walkers elbowing their way past the slow, never mind the No Overtaking signs.

This fitness walking is a good bit less demanding than even race walking (more elegant, too). The only rules are that you do it regularly, no less than three times a week, and for at least 30 minutes or more each occasion, at a good old pace. Of course as a beginner you don't have to start off so strictly, especially if you regard yourself as rather decrepit. You have to put in *some* effort though, so get on to the full schedule soon – and keep your sessions continuous. Don't stop to shop!

Nevertheless, walking in the country is going to remain the most delightful way to heart-strengthening aerobics, so onwards to the rambling boom! In Britain there's a campaign afoot to force a change in the law so that peaceful walkers may go where they please on any farmer's land, not just along our present public footpaths, sometimes 'accidentally' mislaid by the farmers. This is not so barmy a plan; in Sweden it's law already; you may even pitch your tent anywhere you like overnight, without caring about archaic property 'morality'. The air and land belong to all (OK, let them get on with their farming).

Here's a measure of the energy used in walking. If you walk an hour at 6 mph – that's *fast* – it matches the energy requirement from a tennis match. At 4 mph, you're doing the equivalent of normal cycling speed. But 3 mph is no more vigorous than bowls. You then find an hour is the least session you could get away with. It worked out that for each hour a Harvard alumnus exercised he gained an hour of life.

23

GARDENING
Health and beauty by the acre

For centuries gardening has been granted a kindly pat on the head as being very, very *good* for one. Kipling promised you glory from the garden 'once your back stops aching and your hands begin to harden', and Voltaire was quite patronizing too.

But it's only lately that gardening has been elevated to the ranks of real exercise, the Health Education Council having set up a major study of its values and effects.

Professor Jerry Morris, world pioneer in fitness studies, is now analyzing the statistics collected and believes the major benefits are likely to be shown as increased mobility, the burning up of calories, the handling of stress and a certain amount of vigorous working of the large muscle groups. It is vigorous work that produces endurance fitness, the most important aspect in keeping the heart trim.

Note then that the more vigorously you undertake gardening the greater the benefit to the heart. Keep going good weather and bad – wrapping up well can almost turn the bad into good again – and don't stop too often to lean on the spade. Contrariwise, you may certainly take on as many mechanical assistants as you please, for then you will be able to make a more beautiful garden, getting the extra exercise through extending yourself over a larger canvas, as it were.

The disabled gain greatly by this thinking for there are special mechanical aids now developed that enable them to do real gardening, to work hard at it, and thus get the benefit of

---

GARDEN RUBBISH

★ More than 1000 gardeners a year end up in casualty departments as a result of secateur accidents.

★ Gardeners are a hardy perennial species. Sir David Scott, diplomat and gardener, was buried recently aged 99.

★ World record weight for a pumpkin: 612 lb, the weight of four grown men.

★ Many garden accidents involve young children who tuck into slug pellets, ant-powder and berries.

★ The fourth largest cause of accidents in gardens is the deck chair. Sit down at your peril!

Gardening as therapy

For many people gardening is a life-long interest, an activity they find relaxing, stimulating and worthy to share with others through gardening clubs, flower shows and societies. Those who think they can no longer enjoy this interest because they are too old or disabled can take heart from Horticultural Therapy, an organization that concentrates on therapeutic and rehabilitative programmes for the elderly and the handicapped. They offer a range of activities including sessions on Developing and Running a Gardening Therapy Programme and provide services to help the gardener with special needs.

They also provide opportunities for people to meet and exchange ideas, plants, recipes and seeds. There are tools that can be adapted for gardeners with lifting and other difficulties, and opportunities for contact with young people through many of the projects.

Contact: Horticultural Therapy, Goulds Ground, Vallis Way, Frome, Somerset.

exercise. At the other extreme, even athletes find gardening can supplement their work-outs, especially in flexibility. There is no doubt of the tremendous value. It's possibly the finest way to combine health and enjoyment, for the newest of new-marrieds and for the oldest of the elderly, keeping those who are retired in with a motive. At the lower end of the age scale, start children off with a lifelong interest by giving them a plot of their own to work on. Planting an acorn now, they'll see a gnarled aged oak standing there by the time they reach 100.

Even those without a garden of their own can benefit. Apply for an allotment! They're available in most parts. Or create a world record in window-box displays . . . or set up an immense indoor park. Enter the gardening or allotment shows run by local clubs or societies. It will help with stress, at the very least, and further may make you so enthusiastic a gardener that you seek out wider landscapes. Visit the local garden centre or spend a day at a public garden or stately home.

Hazards of gardening:
- Injuring a foot. Wear solid shoes or boots.
- Electric shock from mowers, etc. Buy implements with safety cut-outs.
- Tetanus, from bacteria in the soil that get into open wounds. Make sure you have an anti-tetanus jab, clean up all cuts.
- Back trouble. Dig with a straight back.

YOGA
The two-way exercise

Yoga is both spiritual and physical exercise. Our Western psyche will distinguish between the physical and spiritual planes, but for a true disciple of yoga such a distinction is irrelevant and useless. However, a Westerner may not wish to explore the spiritual universe of the Yogi, and yet obtain a good deal of benefit to health in mind and body from this relaxing form of exercise.

The range of yogic disciplines available, and the curious language used, can put off the casual enquirer. Don't be afraid. It's not that difficult, and you can involve yourself as much as you want. Some people are happy to do no more than attend an evening class once a week for the sake of the fitness that they could gain; others will find themselves drawn in deeper. It's up to you.

Books and teachers can help. Many local authorities offer yoga classes, and libraries stock a selection of texts.

Yoga, for all its cosmic implications, exists *within* the world. It calls for a clean and peaceful environment. You would not expect to find a yogi assuming the lotus position in the middle of a traffic jam. For this reason, yogis often seek the comforts of nature – a hillside on the Upper Ganges, perhaps a Yorkshire moor, or a lonely beach in Portugal. Of course most of us must work in towns and cities, but our health may improve if we import a little nature into the concrete jungle.

Yoga and sex go well together. Tantric yoga is a discipline devoted to the fullest expression of the sexual impulse. Love-making becomes a form of divine contemplation, an infinite ritual.

Other activities, too, benefit from yoga. Art and music have reached a high level in places where yogic disciplines are found. Science and mathematics can trace their origins back to a time when the founders of yoga developed their subtle craft.

Many yoga postures are inspired by nature: e.g. The Swaying Palm, The Flying Swan and The Hare. (Some have been 'borrowed' by lay coaches of fitness or dance.) Careful observation of natural phenomena, such as the sleeping positions of the domestic cat, will educate the student in the natural ways. Consider, too, the energy of trees and fish. These have much to show about the forms and movements of what is called 'chi', or life-energy.

Patience and calmness are both the requirements and rewards of yoga. Take your time, find a quiet space and the benefits will flow.

10

SWIMMING
Sport of all trades

Swimming has values for many different sports and for basic fitness enthusiasts – not to mention for swimmers themselves! Swimmers form a very large proportion of the country's participants in sport, yet interestingly, 98 per cent of them pursue it mainly as a recreational exercise, and never swim in competition.

Meanwhile competitors from other sports wade in and get supplementary training through swimming. Running and cycling elite performers often find extra aerobic training by doing many hours in the water in addition to their mileage on the roads or track. They also switch over to swimming entirely at times, when injury to the legs requires them to lay off running with its hard impact, to keep their cardio-respiratory level and morale up to scratch. Then of course there are the triathletes, who combine running and cycling with swimming as the basis of their sport.

This is all a tribute to the healthfulness and safety of swimming. An ideal sport, therefore, for anyone still lurking on the edge of decision. Swimming helps flexibility, muscle tone, strength and stamina, as well as heart-and-lung capability. Because your body is supported by the water you are less likely to strain any muscles through using incorrect techniques. On top of that it's become a byword for dealing with stress and city fatigue. And don't forget the recreational value, which after all is what appeals to so many already.

Take the plunge, get in the swim

There are 1200 public pools in Great Britain, many with local authority adult swimming classes. Learning to swim is simple – and essential.

The Swim Fit programme, developed by the Amateur Swimming Association, is for both learning and improving. It includes skill-teaching for distances right up to 500 miles. That should do as a target!

Contact: The Association at Harold Fern House,
Derby Square,
Loughborough,
Leicestershire.

(They'll also supply details of special antenatal, parent and baby classes.)

27

There are two kinds of dangerous stress: acute and chronic. Acute stress, such as you might feel in a car crash, or at a football match, is fortunately rare. It can, however, hurt you badly – shock alone will stop the heart. Obviously, we all try and avoid acute stress, with the aid of our common sense and survival instincts. A few seconds' extra thought in traffic, a few minutes' patience after Liverpool have lost – take your time and you'll win more time.

Most of what we call stress in our society is chronic. The great common traumas include the aching heart after bereavement or divorce, as well as the new job or the new house. Then there are those daily stresses: the constant thudding of the neighbours' stereo; anxiety about the phone bill. These are the things that gradually wear down the will to live, that injure the arteries and wind up the nerves. And they don't just go away overnight. There's always another bill to pay, another sleepless night of yearning for a departed mate.

Tears may bring relief, but they won't clean up the milk. At some stage you've got to take positive action, get out of the house and on to the street all alone. You won't find a new lover sitting by the telephone, but you might find one at the local disco or lolling about on a Spanish beach. And if love no longer holds you in its thrall, you'll still have to admit the need for friendship. Where are your new pals? They might be at work, or they might be in the swimming pool. You can be sure they won't be knocking on your door, any more than you might be knocking on theirs.

The practical approach is the only approach. Take noise, for instance. The more you complain, the more you'll alienate the folks next door. One day *you* might want to have a party – just imagine what they'll have to say then.

Life is full of rhythms, some fast and some slow. Sages and peasants agree: tune yourself into these rhythms, find time and space for contemplation, and many of your problems will gradually recede. For all the extraordinary technical advances, we're still just animals, living, breathing creatures. Use the machines, but don't turn into one.

11

STRESSORS
The imbalance of forces

Stress kills. In its acute mode, such as shock, it can induce heart failure. Chronic stress may contribute significantly to the big killers: heart attack, stroke and cancer. In heart attack and stroke, for instance, the damage is done when the coronary and cerebral arteries are clogged up by atheroma. It may be that stress on the heart and head encourages this clogging-up.

Stressors – the things that stress you – vary from one environment to another. In rural India traffic noise is no great problem, but food anxiety can be deadly serious. Living next door to a nuclear power station, no doubt, will cause great stress – even more so if you're also worried about unemployment. Families are notorious stressors, but can also be great soothers. Love stresses, but where would we be without it?

Stress in moderation can be good for you. Overwork generates great symphonies, scientific achievements and sporting feats. Push yourself harder; you often find you can do things you'd never dream possible. Once again, the needs vary with the individual. It's a balancing act.

But beware. Modern society is highly stressful and many of us are likely to be damaged. To complicate it, the evils may not show up for years. A healthy man is carried off by a brain tumour; a woman in the bloom of life is mercilessly struck down by breast cancer. It's more than likely that stress has played a part. Years of overwork, emotional and sexual repression, a harsh environment – they can shorten life dramatically. Face up to stress *now* – recognize the symptoms and partake of the cures.

Tricks to relieve stress

★ Country walks. Nothing like the birds, the trees and a lungful of fresh air. Country runs: ditto.

★ A modest nip. A gin and tonic after work often hits the right button.

★ Relaxation techniques. Yoga, meditation, Alexander, deep breathing.

★ Music. The fiddle was favoured by Sherlock Holmes and Albert Einstein. A drum kit can be fun if your neighbours are deaf.

★ Chopping wood. Though when you burn it you're polluting the atmosphere even more.

12

BEREAVEMENT
Coping with the greatest sorrow

Studies show that the shock and grief of a bereavement increase your own chances of death and disease. Most people know this instinctively, but rational knowledge does not always help when the blow falls. Letting your grief flow out, neither stifling nor hurrying it, is the way to soften the blow, and *it must be done*. Facing up to and dealing with bereavement will lengthen your life – it may even strengthen it in a subtle fashion. As Dora Russell said: 'You look around and see the plants and animals die. So why not live!'

The first year is the worst. Colin Murray Parkes, in his invaluable book *Bereavement*, identifies three major factors: grief, stigma and deprivation. All three hit hardest in the first year, so that's the time when you should take greatest care of yourself. *GRIEF* is as unique as love – some people call it the price of love. Yet there are underlying patterns and feelings we all have to deal with. Anger, guilt, shock, resentment, pining and sorrow lead finally to resolution. It may take two years or it may take ten. All you can do with grief is feel it and try to communicate your feelings to others. Don't hold back the tears – there's

---

FACTS AND CUSTOMS

★ Bereavement has been blamed as a contributory factor in the causes of leukaemia, ulcerative colitis, asthma and many psychiatric conditions.

★ A former practice among Jews was for the eldest unmarried brother to marry the deceased's widow. This is know as 'Levirate' marriage.

★ When the film idol Rudolph Valentino died, public grief was such that some women committed suicide.

★ The Shuswap people of British Columbia have a strong taboo on bereaved people. Among other ordeals, they must bathe regularly, rub their bodies with spruce and sleep on thorn bushes.

★ Suttee, the practice of immolation of widows on the funeral pyres of their husbands, was first mentioned in the first century BC. It was banned in India by the British in 1829. Some women were burnt prior to the husband's expected death in battle.

Your loss – and winning through

Your primary concern is looking after *yourself* – maintain the continuity of life. When the mourning is over deliberately set about to re-engage in your job and your other activities, more intensively than before.

When in doubt talk about your suffering to others – don't bottle it up. No stiff upper lip is wanted!

If you've lost your spouse, take a part-time course or get some friendly consultation on carrying out the practical duties of your late partner. Men: study housework; women: learn to be the man-about-the-house. You can reduce problems to come by writing a will that leaves your affairs tidy.

nothing like a good cry, however tough you may think you are.

Talk to anybody: your doctor, a psychiatrist, ministers of religion, Samaritans, friends, family, bereavement groups and barmen. In a sense, it's everybody's problem, and most people are sympathetic at heart. It's better to feel foolish than bitter.

Ritual mourning, such as the Catholic wake or Jewish shivah, is often of great help. Don't just dismiss these ancient traditions, though don't follow them if you don't want to and can find your own way of grieving.

STIGMA results from people's fear of their own feelings. Bereavement groups can be particularly helpful here. In a group, all are equal in grief. Ask your GP about groups.

DEPRIVATION, or secondary loss due to a bereavement, can be severe. A widow may lose her income or her home, company and sexual fulfilment. A widower may be unable to cook and clean adequately. An orphaned child may suffer many other material losses.

There is no easy answer for deprivation. In other cultures the extended family often cares for the bereaved; in our society much of the care comes from the state and the individual. Perhaps the most important practical step one can take is to learn self-reliance. In addition, the cultivation of other loving relationships, in a word, friends, can ease the pangs and fears.

To protect your physical health, you should bear in mind that bereavement is often followed by an increase in the consumption of tranquillizers, alcohol and tobacco, and by a decline in appetite and sexual feeling. Determine not to let these affect you.

Lastly, even if you haven't been bereaved yourself, it won't hurt to help others. Listen to their sorrow, invite them to dinner, give them a ring. You'll find it pays off.

13

THE 3-LETTER MYSTERY
Clue – it's today's saddest unsung malady

What is the most common, most frequent, most dreaded malady to affect our population? And the least played-up?

Not the common cold. Clue: as a mass attacker it's newer than the century. Another: it can predispose towards stress, accident-proneness, hysteria, depression, divorce and suicide; furthermore there is no known treatment, and – wait for it – it touches only half of the population.

By now that half will have guessed ... it's PMT, premenstrual tension. The other half doesn't completely realize the miserable way it grips a part of the female population. For younger ones it can be an unpleasant introductory shock and for the rest, fifteens to fifties, a recurring period of stress, where often they feel changes to their personality are being wreaked by some inside poison, accompanied by quite savage pain.

It's a modern complaint that has stealthily crept up on civilization. Until after World War I women in the mass had not experienced the menstrual period month after month, not enough to assess what it was really like. In primitive societies they had nursed their young until the age of two or three, during which time there was no menstruation to endure, so no Pre. In Victorian times woman began the family in her teens and kept at it, year after year, infant after infant, to fill in the measure of her days until over 40 and nearing the menopause, the end of her fertility. Hardly a moment left for enduring menstruation, nor

---

WHAT VICTIMS HAVE SAID

Joan R: I am seized by crippling pain and mental blackouts and am completely unable to help myself.

RRW: I never know what's hit me until it is happening. Then I change personality, something chemical happens to me.

GC: Why stop smoking – I couldn't care less about myself and my future, life like this is not worth living.

SMC: My black visitor.

SJS: I'm like a monster. I get fits of uncontrollable temper. A doctor: It lies behind criminal offences. It can destroy careers.

Note: **Ask** any five acquaintances, to see just how many genuine victims there are.

---

again PMT. And who was it therefore who turned out to be the querulous character of Victorian literature? The spinster, the childless woman, of course.

The normal adult woman each month goes through a cycle of powerful hormonal changes, evolved over millions of years to provide the best ambience for procreation. Evolution did not worry about the negative effects on any rare woman who might decide against the norm of permanent motherhood. Because the vogue of having fewer babies is comparatively modern, medical science may perhaps be able to excuse itself for not yet having given the problem enough major attention. Until this very day there are family doctors who will do nothing but tell a patient that she has to 'learn to live with it'. It's true that no universally effective treatment is available, yet some women can be helped by vitamin B6 and some by that romantic-sounding potion, oil of evening primrose.

Those women who have benefited from B6, or pyridoxine, pass on advice to others that patience and a sense of experiment are needed when trying it out. It will certainly take months to become fully effective and in addition you have to find out by trial and error at just what part of the cycle you give yourself the tablets, and precisely how much of a dose.

As scientific research has not come up with a satisfactory answer for all, alternative therapy has moved into this area. So far: no substantial success.

Women thus, many of them, still endure a few black days each month. There are those who will bury themselves for a day or two in bed, but this is little help; it doesn't reduce the pain, or the feeling of hopelessness or the incidence of family rows that may be generated, and it doesn't even assist in concealing the misery from themselves, no more than the ostrich-like burying of the head.

Determination and building up your valuation of yourself – *not* self-abnegation – are the best ways of getting through the critical time. Or perhaps you might set down in big letters in your diary, the day or so before PMT becomes due: 'I know I may hit it tomorrow, I know I'll think there's something wrong with me and that it's all my fault and that the whole miserable world is no good – BUT I'M NOT GOING TO BELIEVE IT! HERE IS MY DECLARATION.' Prepare yourself, defend yourself against it.

And make further efforts to get the best advice through your GP on how to cure yourself.

PMT varies in its force and viciousness, perhaps with your state of health, physical or mental, and of course it varies in its effects from person to person. One thing that can be said, though, is that it never hits the male of the species – not directly, though he may well suffer the backlash of it. Is it because of this that PMT gets less than its fair share of understanding and application from the men of medicine?

14

DIVORCE
After the break

Divorce is a most painful disturbance, second highest to the death of a spouse on the Richter scale of life's earthquakes. The fissures and faults of its upheaval create not only emotional and practical problems but strike damagingly at the heart. It is life-threatening to both partners – reason enough for further efforts to keep the marriage going. Have you been to the Marriage Guidance people? Have you thought out the grave consequences of divorce? There is no winner; trauma is in store even for the one who may be eyeing the champagne.

Only if determined attempts to benefit from counsel fail should you continue the divorce process. Then decide at all costs to manage an amicable divorce, for this will help limit the harm to your heart, emotionally and physiologically.

Thereafter there is much to be said for a clean break; clinging to the partnership will not help you establish a new life nor heal the old, and your future health and happiness will be affected. If you hang around your old partner hoping that he or she may yet come back to you, you're not giving yourself a chance of finding a new person. And if you're the one walking off with a new partner, stay away from your old. Play fair, give the old spouse a chance, don't keep her or him on a string for your own convenience – nor make the mistake of thinking you're being of help; it's kinder to be cruel.

Of course where the break is mutual a continuing friendship between former spouses has positive pay-offs, particularly for

---

FACT BOX

★ The average length of marriage until divorce is only 10 years.

★ Women are twice as likely to divorce after a second marriage as after a first.

★ The re-marriage rate for men is nearly three times as high as that for women.

★ A Johannesburg couple were married and re-married to each other five times.

★ Spouses who marry in their teens are almost twice as likely to divorce as those who marry in their early twenties.

How to help yourself

In *Coping with Separation and Divorce*, Ann Mitchell has this advice for the newly divorced:

Keep a diary of your daily feelings, it will help you get them in perspective. You also have a record of your progress.

Become involved in community activities to help get you out of yourself.

Have a good cry, preferably in the company of a friend.

If you need to share your experience with others in the same boat, join the National Council for the Divorced and Separated.

Don't be afraid to lean on family and friends as temporary props, but avoid other people's spouses!

If you are a one-parent family join Gingerbread, which provides support for single parents and their children.

the children. Certainly you should speak no ill of your old partner, for after all you have shared a life together and it would be seen as no more than a slur on yourself. Slanging others serves but to hurt your own inner peace.

Your feelings will range from anxiety, anger, regret, despair and depression to grief, guilt, loneliness and loss of self-esteem. Regard these as short-term afflictions only; time and taking charge of your life will distance you from their intensity. There may also be a tremendous sense of relief; there is the opportunity to make changes that were formerly constrained by the relationship. You can please yourself, sing at midnight, dance till dawn, and, unless you have children, the only demands on your time are your own.

It is important to establish an identity as a single person after the break. Many young divorcees rush into a subsequent marriage because they have only existed as a couple. Beware of embarking on a serious relationship while still recovering emotionally from your divorce. Your next partner should not be regarded as a consolation prize or you will be following one mistake with another.

Take the separation in two stages. Make short-term decisions first. Do not move out of a familiar environment. As an interim arrangement stay with family or friends. When self-esteem and confidence are restored start making the long-term decisions that are going to have a permanent effect on your life. Remember that you have made an important decision to change your life; as you fold away the decree absolute, you have elected to enter a new phase, full of choice and change.

15 MOVING-DAY TRAUMAS
Ours is a nice 'ouse ours *was*

Completion at noon. Here we were at 11 am, the pantechnicon with our household goods by now at our new house a mile away, the invading pantechnicon already at our front gate ... sprawled all over it. We had to stop the men from trundling in The Enemy's chattels before the legal moment for possession.

Then, while we were wolfing apples from the garden (it still belonged to us at that moment), The Enemy came on the phone. The Enemy – the incoming owners – snivelled on about how we had unrightfully removed a built-in fitting. It was specifically included in the contract of sale, they claimed.

'No!' said we, shocked, 'What fitting?' There were *hundreds* of fittings we had thrown in, generous considering the small-minded way they had bargained down the price.

We had to interrupt the call to answer a loud knocking. At the gate there was now a second pantechnicon, double-parked outside the first, and blocking the street. It was a familiar van: ours.

'They says at yer new 'ouse they ain't not yet ready, yer can't move in today,' said our driver. 'What I done is, I come back 'ere then,' the genius added. We were aghast! Noon today was completion time, right up and down the chain. It seemed the hold-up at our new house was through the departing Bandits there not being able to yank a Dutch stove out of the wall. 'What!' We screamed at the driver: what did he mean, that stove had been advertised in the particulars of sale and was on

---

TALL STOREYS AND HOME TRUTHS

★ Over 60 per cent of the British population own their own homes.

★ For the majority of people a new house is the largest personal financial transaction they will make in their lives.

★ In Great Britain 50 per cent of all adults have lived in their homes for more than 10 years.

★ In the United States it is a common sight to see mobile homes being transported from one place to another on trucks.

Handy hints on houses

1 Be particularly considerate to your children before the move, and on the day leave young children and animals with friends or relatives overnight.
2 Make lists of everything you have to do before, on and after the move. Include everything you want to throw out, give away or sell.
3 Use a reputable removal firm with plenty of packers.
4 Beware of back strain. Get medical advice on how to lift correctly.
5 Make sure you have an agreed list with the purchasers of everything you are leaving in the old house and garden.
6 To help yourself get established in your new area find out where the doctor, hospital, bank and police are.
7 Introduce yourself to your new neighbours and ask about local services and deliveries.

no account to be yanked out and taken away?

Back to our telephone conversation to inform The Enemy moving in that they could see their lawyers about the fitting. We weren't giving in to petty blackmail.

The driver nagged on: 'Where to offload this lot?' he asked. 'WHAT!' He had another job for the van next day, he said stolidly. We now tried to telephone The Bandits ahead of us in the chain to warn them to get moving, without the stove, but their phone was already disconnected.

So we instructed our lawyers to threaten The Bandits that we would not complete at all if they did not admit us and our belongings immediately. We also briefed them to threaten the other lot, The Enemy, that we would not hand over our house at all if they kept up their absurd claim on our spice-rack, which was the 'built-in fitting' they coveted, and never mind that the party behind them in the chain had already arrived in *their* pantechnicon and were half moved into The Enemy's old house. The Enemy could set up life in their van for all we cared.

Yes, we thought, perhaps it would be better to cancel both sales and stay on in our own very nice old house after all. . . .

The lawyers managed to separate us by mid-afternoon and late at night the whole chain was moved along one and rehoused. We needed a lie-in for two days, with heavy tranquillizers for two months to follow, to recover from the trauma and stress. And we had to finance the purchase of a new spice-rack as well as a new stove, plus lawyer's bills. It happens even to the nicest people on moving day.

16 SOUND POLLUTION
Noises on and off

At 180 decibels sound can kill; at 200 it becomes a horrific military weapon. Even at lower levels, 120 to 130, as experienced beneath a low-flying aircraft, it can cause pain to humans and animals. It was an RAF fighter that ruined the sex life of a billy goat, through scaring the poor animal out of its socks while at stud. The RAF was obliged to pay the owner damages, based on Billy's fee of £70 per session.

Noise, even at 65db, its effect in a busy street, can be very much the opposite of life-enhancing. You can suffer disturbance from a mere 30db, the relentless ticking of a watch beneath your pillow.

It's usually other people's noise, which we can't control, that causes misery, and as the total amount of it in the world creeps upwards, due to the increasing density of modern traffic – coupled with the decreasing thickness of modern walls – and the growth in the amplifying power of modern hi-fi, we are coming around to the necessity for dealing with it. In Britain the Noise Abatement Society has made great advances: through its efforts we have been saved from the threat of talking posters, have had

---

BIG NOISES

★ Prolonged exposure to high noise levels can cause permanent deafness – while 150 decibels will do the trick immediately.

★ Noises of around 85 decibels can cause irritability, heartburn, indigestion, ulcers, high blood pressure and possibly heart disease.

★ Bursts of noise are known to alter endocrine, neurological and cardiovascular functions in the human body.

★ Some discos operate at 130 decibels, louder than the accepted level of tolerance.

★ The ultimate in noise pollution is an artificially manufactured sound of 210 decibels, capable of boring holes in solid material.

★ Possibly the loudest bang was caused by the eruption of Krakatoa in Indonesia. When the volcano erupted in 1883, the explosions were heard 2200 miles away in Australia.

---

noisy factories brought to task and have been provided with an Aircraft Hotline Service (01-633 3001) that is helping to ensure the survival of the goat population among others.

The society awards the Seal of Silence to firms whose products are well sound-insulated and it publicizes to all the fact that noise is ugly, wasteful and the cause of damage to the perpetrators as well as to others. That's putting a great deal of faith in the power of advice and example. But how else do you get it across to a motor-biker who enjoys stripping off his silencer for the exhilarating feeling it gives him? The law is inadequate. Or to the youngster carrying a large stereo that has no silencer to start with?

It is these kind of domestic sounds that are at the heart of the problem. Last year the unfortunate award of Public Complaint Number One in the charts went to Neighbour Noise!

One of the objectives the anti-noise faction are pushing for is the setting-up of a Quiet Room in each household. They also want a right to acoustic privacy for all citizens.

Naturally, campaigns like this often run contrary to other interests. Barking dogs, the objects of bitter hatred at one end of the street, are considered by their owners at the other to be acting very properly as watchguards. A difficult area, requiring a Solomon to sit in judgement when controversy arises.

Less difficult to condemn are the public address systems at airports. Not satisfied with having planes buzzing about noisily outdoors, the world's terminals all employ people to fill the air indoors with further sound garbage, sending out muffled calls such as: 'Passengers on BA One Thousand, to South Bewilderness, your plane has already left'. Or so it sounds, for all the use it is. So too with announcements in railway stations – their only value, that they might be helpful to the blind (those with perfect hearing at any rate).

What can the individual do to protect his hearing and sanity from attacks of noise pollution? Available from the noise abatement people are ear defenders, which can knock 60db off the sound level, ear plugs proper and home soundproofing kits. An Italian textile manufacturer has recently developed a highly effective means of soundproofing; this involves weaving a fabric from textile and lead. It is lighter than lead alone, and more flexible than lead, making it more versatile and yet cheaper. Look for it on the market before long. (Meanwhile avoid taking aspirin for headaches brought on by noise pollution, as too much of that can cause ringing in the ears).

To keep you from contributing to the noise level yourself, there is the silent dog whistle. With it you can blow to your heart's content, whereupon the animal, which has the ability to hear its exceptionally high-frequency tone, will come to heel, while the human population can carry on regardless.

17 THE MENOPAUSE
. . . and overcoming it

'Menopausal care is one of the most important forms of preventive medicine in the twentieth century.'

John Studd, Consultant, Dulwich Hospital

As a woman you no longer need fear the menopause. Today there is plenty you can do to help yourself through this sometimes tearful and trying experience. There are clinics, counselling services and self-help groups to provide medical advice and emotional support. Understanding what is happening and taking a positive attitude will help alleviate the symptoms. Self-knowledge will also help people bear with you.

What are the symptoms, what happens to your body? The menopause or climacteric normally occurs around the age of 50, in the following three stages:

Pre-menopause: starts 3–10 years before your periods stop and includes irregular periods, the first definite symptoms, mood changes and hot flushes in the week of the period.

Peri-menopause: the stage when your periods stop; your last period signifies the menopause.

Post-menopause: follows on immediately after the above. The three most important effects are hot flushes, vaginal dryness and osteoporosis (thinning of the bones).

The ovaries now become less active and the adrenal glands continue the production of small amounts of oestrogen essential

---

TAKE NOTE AND PAUSE

★ A heavy smoker is likely to have an early menopause.

★ Osteoporosis is the most common metabolic bone disease in the western world.

★ You lose about 1 per cent of bone a year after the menopause, faster if you have had your ovaries removed.

★ The chances of osteoporosis at age 50 are 1 in 20; at age 60, 1 in 4 and age 70, 1 in 2.

★ Menopause lowers the risk of some forms of cancer (eg: cancer of the cervix).

★ Women are the only animal species apart from apes in captivity to undergo the menopause.

Helping yourself

★ Get up early – lying in bed thins the bones.

★ Have regular dental and medical check-ups.

★ Take contraceptive precautions for two years if your last period occurred under 50, for one year if you are over 50.

★ Pelvic exercises and regular sexual activity counteract vaginal dryness and thinning of the vaginal wall.

★ Try yoga and swimming for the relief of stress and irritability.

★ Help skin with moisturizers, add oil to your bath, wear protective creams for sport and weather.

★ Give up smoking. The risk of a heart attack from smoking is quadrupled after the menopause if you are a heavy smoker.

to maintaining calcium in the bones. The adrenal glands thrive on stimulation so it is vital to take regular exercise. This, coupled with a calcium enriched diet, discourages osteoporosis.

Bad flushes can be eased with regular tepid showers (avoid hot baths) and the elimination of alcohol, spicy foods and coffee from your diet. Wear cotton bras and layers of loose cotton clothing. Vaginal dryness is improved with sexual activity – masturbation even – aided if necessary by a commercial lubricant or oestrogen tablets.

Take up a new occupation, new creative interest or new partner if necessary – this helps maintain an alert mind and well-tuned body, which will increase longevity. It's thanks to an enterprising spirit continuing into their seventies and eighties that people like Dame Freya Stark, the traveller and writer, have kept young so long. Dame Freya went down the Euphrates at 83 and is still enjoying life in her nineties.

Between the ages of 40 and 50 some men experience the 'male menopause', a misnomer for an emotional crisis that lasts about four years. They feel an imperative and irrational need for change coupled with coming to terms with physical deterioration. Some experience temporary impotence, which can be treated with a course of testosterone. Again the prescription is diet, exercise, cutting down on alcohol and avoiding cigarettes. Talk to your partner or a friend about your restlessness.

Couples going through the menopause at the same time can share diet and exercise programmes (try new ways of sexual fulfilment) and give each other support.

18

SLEEP
Where sheep may safely graze

Never mind Rip Van Winkle, there are people with us today who have spent as much as 35 years asleep. For of course at eight hours a day of sleep you're into double figures by the time you're 30. The easy-going set who are fond of an afternoon nap as well might get a good 40 years of sleep in by the time they receive their 100th birthday greeting from the Palace.

Think how much more they might have crammed in could they have utilized that time . . . another one or two careers.

Still, this takes no account of the prime function of sleep, the deliberate whiling away of time during the night hours so that the body may replenish and recover.

SOPORIFICA

★ Although sleep is a time of rest, it is also a time of repair and growth; some tissues, such as epitheleum, actually proliferate more rapidly during sleep.

★ Sleep deprivation can result in changes in personality and of perceptual and intellectual processes.

★ Sleeping drugs tend to reduce the amount of dreaming-type sleep, one reason for their long-term use being regarded as harmful.

★ The study of sleep has identified two distinct types of sleep: S sleep which occupies 75 per cent of the time spent sleeping and D sleep, also called paradoxical sleep because the nervous system is very active, occupying 25 per cent of the time sleeping.

★ During D sleep, essential to the body's well being, your brain allows thoughts to be processed.

★ Snoring is not essential to satisfying sleep; it is induced by lying on one's back or as a result of enlarged adenoids or a sagging pharynx.

★ Some people claim to require no sleep at all, but when tested are found to have very short snatches of D sleep – missing out the S sleep completely.

★ Sleep is normally regarded as restorative to the body, though medical conditions such as angina may be accentuated by the conditions of sleep.

The unanimous verdict for most animal species is that you really need the balmy ministrations of sleep. It's the opinion of the individual too. Given the chance many of us would lie in for hours longer if there weren't a job of work to do. The head of the animal kingdom, the lion, won't allow such petty thoughts to disturb him; after a good meal he will snore away for days, until his stomach demands a refill . . . then the chase is on.

Sleep, and the need for it, has been the subject of intense scientific study in recent years. There is a distinguished body of scientists who attend regular conferences on the subject (doubtless with carefully planned rest periods between sessions). A radical notion presented at one of these conferences was that it was *sleep* that was the natural state of being, not arousal. There are many who would agree. The theory was that waking and moving around were gradually added on to a normally somnolent pattern of animal behaviour.

However lying too long abed is a refuge for those of us who are depressed, rather than fatigued. You bury your head so that you may forget about how hard the world is treating you. It is your guilt you are burying, in reality. The paradox is that a depressed patient might first be advised to benefit from a restful period, but it will then be up to the doctor to coax him into a full programme of life's activities.

Those who are stressed, as opposed to depressed, often find it hard to get in the proper quota of sleep, 'nature's soft balm'. This is where sheep and tranquillizers may be needed . . . counting the former and counting the cost of the latter, for as always with drug-taking you pay back in side-effects.

It is the notorious Type A personality, the aspiring and over-ambitious, who is most likely to be found battling for enough sleep. The head may be on the pillow, but the mind is still racing around. Even heavy physical activity such as weight-lifting undertaken too soon before sleep leaves the brain over-stimulated; there is an excess of oxygen in the blood flowing around the system to keep the brain stirred up.

The solution for both these hyperactive types is to spend an hour or so at some calm occupation before retiring, something like crossword puzzling, quite unproductive – it needs to be, for as soon as you attempt to make it unwasteful and even profitable you'll be back again on the ambition trail.

Whether you need to adjust your amount of sleep upwards or downwards, you should tailor the general advice available to suit yourself. For some people coffee is no problem, for instance, while others dare not take a cup later than midday if they want to sleep well that night. Work out your own routines on this as well as on other ways of combating stress or depression, whichever might be your poison. If you straighten out your nights, you'll get your days right too.

19

POLLUTION
Do as you would be done by

Man-made pollution has killed millions. Cholera and TB are the direct result of adverse living conditions – too little space and too much filth. When humans first started living by rivers they used them as toilets. The next thing that happened was that the tribe downstream got sick. So *they* moved upstream, and passed it back to the first tribe. And so on.

Major advances in health have been due to pollution control, particularly of water. Sewage is a subject usually swept under the carpet, so to speak, yet it is of such importance that historians consider it *the* mark of civilization. Early cities of Sumeria and the Indus Valley have evidence of sewage systems, and the Romans, of course, were famed for plumbing.

Clean water is now standard in many countries and on its way in others. But attention in recent years has been directed towards the air: acid rain, ozone depletion, the greenhouse effect, radioactivity. Pollution of the earth is another problem – fertilizers, pesticides, erosion, radiation.

The various elements of our world, or biosphere, are interconnected. The study of these interconnections is called ecology. Wipe out frogs and you encourage the proliferation of insects. Kill trees and the topsoil erodes. Damage the environment and it will damage *you*.

In time humankind will learn to love the world and all its miracles. The cobra has as much right to life as we do. In the meantime we must learn to lessen suffering.

No sane person will deny that pollution is a threat to health, but lessening that pollution is hard. If you abandon driving, you must take the bus, cycle or walk. It's not so convenient or comfortable at 3 am on a wet November's morning. Solar, wind and water energy could provide us with all the electricity we need, but massive capital investment and vested interests favour the present, polluting forms of generation. Energy supply depends not only on available resources but on economics and politics.

There are other obvious ways to reduce pollution. Use less energy: insulate houses, offices, workplaces; improve public transport; buy and grow organic produce; wash less; pressure governments. There are at least 99 ways to handle this threat to life alone. We can be sure we don't know everything about environmental pollution, any more than Elizabethans understood how disease spread, or people of 100 years ago knew about the dire consequences of smog. Education and study still have a role to play in this enterprise.

44

20

THE CASH CRISIS
The root of all evil?

Money and the making of it – and the losing of it! – and the inability to make it at all is of course a main cause of stress, the lurking killer.

In the chain of events money is found to be what the proverb always knew . . . the root of evil. It may seem trite, but money isn't essential, food is; it's food that makes the world go round.

The most civilized of countries, the most sophisticated of classes, the most enterprising of executives . . . that's where you'll find stress and heart attacks. Coronaries and stroke are not generally the fate of your mountain farmer or fisherman. They are the fate of the high pressure – the high-blood pressure – Type A personality, first diagnosed to be at risk in the dollar-driven USA economy. Yes it's primarily the rich that get the heart disease – yet even ordinary people locked into this hectic world suffer stress in their hunt for a living.

Whichever you are, you must deal with the problem. With philosophy, you will learn to keep the pursuit of money strictly in its place. Money is but a small element in the experience of happiness; don't worship it. Regard it with contempt even, so that you can break yourself of its magnetic power.

Pursue it if you must but ask yourself if you *sincerely* want to be rich. The struggle for wealth can overstress and endanger your life.

Bankruptcy, that failure of business action, has slaughtered its thousands, many a once-rich man throwing himself from a skyscraper at the threat of it. Not only may the bankrupt lose his very home on being liquidated, but out goes his life's occupation; in addition he suffers humiliations and slanders. His creditors will claim he has salted his money away, his shareholders will say that he has stolen theirs, and his friends may shun him.

Even the rich and successful are endangered – by the very surfeit of money. It takes away their incentive, adds to their responsibilities and multiplies their worries. What's more it causes them to over-indulge and overeat. Pity the millionaire, who may not walk to work for his own satisfaction, but must drive there, for his chauffeur's. The children of the rich find will-power suffocated by too much of the money they have not earned. Live for the next challenge; climb the mountain that has one peak more.

It is the main fault and fallacy of the western way of life, this adoration of money; to abjure it is the path to a longer and happier time for yourself.

For some reason everyone thinks they know best about food. Hindus never touch beef, while Yorkshiremen eat little else. You will not find a horse steak in England, and a milk pudding very rarely in China. Frenchmen feast on snails, Germans are partial to lung soup.

This is all very natural. The forces of history and culture have led different peoples to different culinary paths. And why not? No doubt there are many species, nutritious and wholesome, that have not yet been tasted by humans. Some obscure Amazonian fruit might prove to be a cure for diabetes. And genetic engineering could add further peculiar dishes to the world table.

None the less, for all the vagaries of taste and opportunity, a rational science of nutrition is emerging. We are now beginning to know which foods will prolong your life and improve your health, and which can be a positive threat. Vitamins have only been identified during this century, but already their crucial importance is recognized. In the case of minerals research is yet more recent. The importance of zinc in the diet, for example, is still a contentious issue.

Food allergies, too, present scientists and lay people alike with much ammunition for debate. Some swear that their allergic status is essential to their health; others pooh-pooh such claims as neurotic and faddish. Many search for definite answers; questions will remain for years to come.

Fats and fibre fill the pages of newspapers and magazines. Hardly a day goes by when the unwary reader is not warned that the pork pie will do him in. Bran-rich cereals, cakes and biscuits are offered as treatment for every disease from acne to Zollinger-Ellison syndrome.

Moderation is counselled by many. Eat less, live longer, they say. And they may be right! Certainly, it looks as though starvation will soon be a thing of the past for the citizens of the world.

Finally, the legion of vegetarians grows daily, their banners unfurled with the motto 'Meat is Murder' emblazoned thereon. It looks as though the Great Food War is far from over.

21

VITAMINS
No shortcut to good health

Whether or not vitamin supplements lengthen and improve your life is a highly debatable question.

There is certainly little evidence of actual clinical vitamin deficiency in Britain. The average GP comes across few serious signs. Lack of folate and B12 might occur occasionally; scurvy less frequently. Doctors with Asian patients quite often deal with cases of rickets – easily treated with Vitamin D.

It seems likely that common sense – regular exercise, meaningful work, decent relationships and relaxation – will be of more benefit than popping vitamin tablets.

Undoubtedly the isolation and understanding of vitamins has been a major medical advance, recognized more than once by the Nobel committee. However, most vitamin research has merely confirmed normality in diet: eat fresh food daily; don't stint on the fruit and vegetables. In the past, access to fresh foods was often limited by transportation, money, war and the weather. This is no longer true for the developed countries. Perhaps our vitamin anxiety is caused by fear of food restriction, memories of war and famine. After all, people still have a sneaking belief in magic potions.

Ironically, strict vegetarians are a group that is at risk of vitamin deficiency. Such people can develop neurological signs of simple B12 deficiency: eyesight trouble, peripheral neuritis, subacute degeneration of the spinal cord and psychological problems. Symptoms are easily remedied with B12 supplement.

For the vast majority of people in the developed countries, a good, varied diet with sunlight should provide all the vitamins ever needed. Half a pound of lightly cooked liver once a week will dispel remaining doubts.

ABC OF VITAMINS

★ The West Indian cherry, or acerola, contains 1000mg of Vitamin C per 100g. This is 50 times as much as oranges and 200 times as much as ordinary cherries.

★ Vitamin A deficiency, resulting in night blindness, was described in Egypt in 1500 BC. Ox liver was the treatment.

★ In 1770 William Stark, a doctor, deliberately induced scurvy in himself for research purposes. He died in the attempt.

THE FIBRE DIET
Take it with a pinch of salt

There is an obsession haunting the land today . . . the worship of the bowel. The fringe medics especially have this notion that the body's channels and tubes need continual sweeping out with bundles of good, wholesome fibre.

To their way of thinking many of our ills can be handled by thus treating what is after all nothing but the garbage department of the human body, the area where, once the 'goodness' has been extracted from food, the residue is stored prior to removal. They enthuse at the 'smooth movements' and peer with approval at the 'floating stools' that fibre produces, inferring from such signs evidence of a healthy system. It is all truly a reading of the entrails as done by the ancients. It is all surely a great moral as well as physical cleansing, a purging of the sin of enjoying too much tasty food. It is all really nothing but a revival of that obsession our grandparents were prone to, the dread of constipation.

The ideal scouring fibre for their purposes is bran. And astonishingly, some even go to the length of prescribing, in the cause of regular bowel movements, bran tablets!

Some fibre is needed in the normal way, of course, it's just that some alternative therapists have gone overboard about it. All sensible people are certainly agreed that a diet of totally

---

FUN WITH FIBRE

★ Pasta, potatoes and bread, once tabooed by dietitians, are now welcomed for their high fibre, weight-reducing content. . . .

★ . . . whereas the Eskimos' natural diet, highly thought of by nutritionists, contains virtually no fibre.

★ Chewing fibre is good for the teeth . . .

★ . . . but too much in the diet may cause heartburn or flatulence.

★ Full of fibre: carrots and celery, and they add few calories. Most other fruit and veg, too, especially rice, lentils, beans, salads. And nuts.

★ In the cooking process heat breaks down fibre in fruit and vegetables; steaming does the least damage.

refined food is inadequate. But – and this is the message – there's no call to worry as long as you tuck into a conventional and rounded set of meals most days, to include fruit and vegetables, of course. You'll then be getting plenty of fibre for your system, and in the natural way.

A simple dressed salad with the main meal will keep you moving well enough! (Not to worry either that the tastiest dressings contain added salt. A pinch or two extra per day is healthily absorbed by normal folk.)

See to it when busy with your fruit intake that you don't discard the fibre with the peels. Apples and pears – bite into them as you find them, skin and all; that's good for the teeth too. Prefer whole-fruit jams for the same reason, they still contain their fibre content.

And peel me no grapes, whatever the song may invite. With oranges and bananas, on the other hand, you're safe enough to chuck away the peels, for there is much fibre in the body of the fruit. Nevertheless, if you have been made nervous by the calls of the fibre-thumpers and want to cover yourself both ways, you'd do no harm to chew through the orange peel too. Raw marmalade, no less!

No, I must admit at least that there isn't any serious harm to be feared from overdoing the fibre; it's simply that its loud and continuous urging takes attention away from getting down to the really effective ways of guarding one's health . . . regular exercise, avoidance of stress and rejection of obesity. That's your big three, remember. Oh, yes, and banning the use of that truly malignant fibre, the tobacco leaf.

23

SUGAR
A sweet reprieve

After decades of banishment sugar is making a sensational comeback. A weighty American government study has been responsible for this shift, through the publication of its report which finds sugar not guilty of damaging the health, except in the matter of tooth decay, and quite innocent of causing fatness.

The influence of this definitive, three-year research project, by a task force of the US Food and Drugs Administration, is still disseminating through the higher levels of health authority, from where it will spread down through doctors and lecturers and over on to television programmes and the pages of women's magazines. In due course it will affect the marketing strategies of food companies, the subsequent supplies to grocers big and small, and the eventual sales to housewives, until habits are gradually changed inside the home. We will eat more sugar – and with fewer guilty feelings.

During its lean years the sugar lobby did its best to beat fashion's ban, resorting sometimes to deception to keep sales up. Here, for instance, is some wily advertising that the sugar companies used: 'A teaspoon of sugar has only 16 calories!' Thus would they clamour on the front of a 1lb sugar package. 'Sugar is the cheapest and best source of energy you can buy!' So they trumpeted immediately below.

SUGAR, NEAT

★ Between the wars sugar-candy was a favourite among children. It was rather like a sugar kebab: a long piece of string dipped in a white sugar solution and crystallized out in large chunks, which could then be gnawed off.

★ Third World kids take their sugar straight from the cane. Having scrumped a length of cane from the fields, they stride along, tearing off the glossy covering with their teeth and chewing the fibre until the sweetness is sucked out of it; then they return it to the land, with a neat spitting action.

★ Sugar and honey have been successfully used for dressing wounds – they can promote rapid and effective healing.

★ A typical person will have eaten enough sugar in a lifetime to fill a London taxi.

. . . on the other hand

Here's a contrary view of the sugar controversy:

Sugar only gives you energy – throw a handful on the fire and see how it flares up. Maybe that's why it's bad for your teeth, the bacteria lap it up.

You won't get minerals, vitamins, protein or other nutrients from sugar.

Also: if there's a tendency in your family you will probably develop diabetes from an excess of sugar, and diabetes, though often un-diagnosed, is a high risk factor for heart attack and stroke.

Contradictory tosh, of course. Energy is *measured in* calories, thus they were wistfully saying that there was not much energy in a teaspoonful of the very thing they were claiming as the best buy in energy.

Now they can let themselves go, since the eminent FDA committee has 'categorically' exonerated sugar of links with blood pressure, diabetes, hyperactivity, heart disease and even obesity.

Of course there were important minority groups who always did maintain that there was no harm in sugar. And the silly fringe faddism of preferring brown sugar had already been disgraced, when scientists had finally got across the point that 'raw' sugar contained exactly the same sucrose as white, but also countless impurities about which much less was known.

It's wonderful how during these past decades fashion was able to cause so much change in eating habits, setting us against sugar – and on flimsy factual evidence. The needless saccharine pills, the superfluous shunning of sweets! The fashionable counting up of calories! Probably even the vogue for slimness itself went well beyond reasonable bounds. This is not to exonerate obesity, a dangerous killer, but to say that there is surely no harm in a little plumpness in men or women, so long as they keep their hearts exercised.

To be fair, fashion is a handy and proper method of spreading information among the population. Now it becomes its task to do right by us and put over the true facts, to assist the nation to ignore fantasies and get on with pinpointing the real agents that damage health. Let us ask for help in this from the sugar industry, which will be crowing now, as will those with a sweet tooth. Perhaps we could ask them to take on, out of gratitude, the sponsoring of other, worthwhile campaigns – there are many more to be found among the 99 Ways.

51

24

FATS AND OILS
Getting rid of extra fat

Yes, the bad news is that excessive consumption of animal/saturated fats may shorten your life. It is believed that **atherosclerosis**, the narrowing and hardening of the arteries, is partly caused by large quantities of animal fat in the diet. And it is atherosclerosis that causes heart attacks and strokes. What's more, it is considered that animal fats may contribute to cancer, particularly of the breast.

The good news: it's possible to eat the most delicious and satisfying meals that are *low* in these potentially lethal fats. A whole new school of cookery has emerged to serve the health-conscious. Use your brain in the kitchen, and you could add to your life-span.

But first get your cholesterol level checked. All it takes is a simple blood test – your GP will happily oblige. Then you'll know if you're at risk, and whether an immediate change of diet is necessary. Some people have a genetic tendency towards a high level of blood cholesterol – hypercholestrolaemia – such people should be particularly careful about fat intake.

Generally speaking, fat is not an essential food. It's true there are some fatty acids which we must have, but the main function of fat is to provide calories for energy. These calories are readily

FAT AND FURIOUS

★ In the early 1970s the average American ate 110 lb of fat a year. In the 1980s the amount was down by an eighth.

★ Fats are digested more slowly than carbohydrates, thus delaying more effectively the feeling of hunger. That's why bread and butter is more satisfying than bread alone, though it is not more nutritious.

★ Cholesterol builds up and causes damage at two major sites: the arteries supplying the brain, and those supplying the heart itself.

★ Generally speaking, countries with a *low* intake of saturated fats and cholesterol, such as Nicaragua, Portugal, Japan and Egypt, have less heart disease than countries with a *high* intake, such as New Zealand, Finland and the USA, although average consumption is dropping all the time.

Ayes and noes

Here's a short list of YES foods and NO foods. YES foods are low in cholesterol and saturated fats; NO foods are high. YES: lean meats, fish, potatoes, skimmed milk, low-fat cheeses, chicken and turkey (without their skins), guavas, mangoes, sweet potatoes, pineapple, peas, green beans, soy beans, mung beans, rice, lentils, watercress, fettucine, tomatoes, spinach, parsnips, turnips, onions, garlic, saffron, prickly pears, courgettes, aubergines, mushrooms, bananas, egg-white, sesame seeds, broccoli, almonds and . . . the list is endless.
NO: egg yolks, butter, cream, lard, bacon grease, chocolate, whole milk, high-fat cheeses (such as Cheddar and Gruyère), and processed products that contain any of them. Plus, of course, meat fat.

available from carbohydrates in our world of plenty. It's true fat also protects against cold, but then again we now have good shelter and heating. It's true that a piece of crackling or a suet pudding is scrumptious . . . but are they worth eating on a daily basis if they pose a threat? You probably needn't worry if your consumption is moderate – what seems to be dangerous is a consistent diet of bacon, eggs, pork pies, sausages and dripping.

More good news: it may be OK to eat fats if your lifestyle is suitable. A person who exercises frequently will be at less risk. Moderate amounts of alcohol seem to help as well. The French have a high-fat diet, but less heart attack and stroke than the British or Americans. Could this be due to their consumption of wine and brandy? Or perhaps it's because they eat more fresh fruit and vegetables. Eskimos eat fat, but also plenty of fish, and have a low incidence of atherosclerosis. Pakistanis always take yoghurt with their fatty meat.

You will be in more danger if you combine a high-fat diet with lack of exercise, plus loads of stress. It's a matter of weighing up one thing against another. If you really can't eliminate animal fats then take up exercise. Ditto if you sit down all day or do a particularly stressful job.

Incidentally, certain oils will actually *lower* your blood cholesterol level. Make sure to partake of these if in any doubt. These include corn, sunflower, peanut, pilchard and whale oils. Just to confuse, there are three *vegetable oils* that raise the cholesterol: coconut, palm and cocoa (found in chocolate).

We'll leave the last word to Duncan 'Tartan Flash' Maclean, the famed international sprinter whose career continued into his nineties: 'I never eat anything that comes out of a frying pan.'

MINERAL INTAKE
Leave it to that expert, the body

There are two types of minerals in the body:
1) Macronutrients – calcium, phosphorus, potassium, sodium, sulphur, chlorine and magnesium.
2) Micronutrients, or trace elements – iron, zinc, selenium, copper, manganese, iodine and others.

They are, of course, all inorganic substances absorbed from food, and used in various processes, and excreted. They vary in quantity from calcium, which makes up about 2 per cent of body weight, to such as cobalt and molybdenum, which exist in

---

MINERAL MATTERS

★ Wilson's disease was once fatal. It is a genetically inherited inability to excrete copper, which builds up in the brain, eyes and other tissues. It responds readily to modern drugs.

★ Chronic zinc deficiency occurs in Iran and Egypt. It results from lack of zinc in the diet; one reason, strangely, is due to a high consumption of wholemeal breads, which prevent available zinc from being absorbed. Symptoms include dwarfism and retarded sexual development.

★ Some people who drink large quantities of red wine suffer from iron overload.

★ Jewish dietary laws forbid the consumption of milk after a meat meal, for six hours. This may result in improved zinc status, as the calcium in milk can interfere with absorption of zinc from the meat.

★ Manganese is an essential trace element. This has been proved by animal experiments. However, manganese deficiency is so rare that the first case was only reported in 1972. Manganese is *toxic* at high levels.

★ Zinc supplements are being investigated as a possible treatment for anorexia. By far the highest source of zinc is the oyster. As zinc is important for reproduction, this may explain the oyster's reputation as an aphrodisiac.

★ Three foods that are particularly high in iron are blueberries, pumpkins and cocoa.

---

amounts so small as only to be measurable by the most sophisticated scientific methods.

Deficiencies of some minerals are well recognized, as are toxicities. Hyperkalemia, too much potassium, can result from kidney failure – and it can kill. Iodine deficiency causes goitre, known as 'Derbyshire neck' because of its one-time frequency in that county.

I say:

Don't worry about your mineral intake, unless you're ill. A modern diet covers most contingencies.

If you do wish to experiment with minerals, adopt a moderate and *balanced* attitude.

It is known that elements in the body exist in competition with, and in balance against, each other. You need sodium to balance the potassium. Cows, whose fodder is potassium-rich, like a salt-lick. Monkeys pick salt flakes from each other to balance the high-potassium bananas on which they thrive. Calcium inhibits your absorption of zinc. There may well be other relationships like these that have not yet been adequately explained.

There has been much recent work on minerals and disease. For instance, platinum compounds are used in cancer chemotherapy, and gold salts in treatment of rheumatoid arthritis. Some recent interesting suggestions, and they're no more than that, have been:

★ Heart disease may be associated with magnesium deficiency.
★ Multiple sclerosis may be influenced by copper deficiency or excess.
★ Fluoride improves teeth, but is chronically poisonous in areas of the world where water contains large quantities.
★ Aluminium poisoning in the Pacific island of Guam causes a fatal neurological illness, amyotrophic lateral sclerosis.

Nevertheless, I still say don't worry about your mineral intake; the body will sort out everything it needs from an ordinary, varied diet. If you do wish to investigate and control your diet the best way is to find out its relevant constituents. There are many good nutritional textbooks, some in local libraries. *The Composition of Foods*, published by Her Majesty's Stationery Office, is a useful tool if you want to check that you are getting all you need from your present diet. But remember that too much can be as harmful as too little.

Bear in mind that you need different things at different times of your life. Pregnant women may need extra zinc; and older women particularly need calcium, to prevent osteoporosis, though it would have been easier for them to absorb their calcium – probably from milk – in their younger days. Vegetarians should pay attention to their mineral status.

FOOD ALLERGY
Disease in disguise?

People thought John Barton had cancer. He was pale, thin and weak; his family and friends were worried. But it turned out that he had coeliac disease, an intestinal sensitivity to the gluten in wheat. Gluten was withdrawn from his diet, and now he is right as rain.

Food allergy may be the root cause behind many health problems. This is being recognized worldwide, albeit reluctantly by doctors – but one must be thankful that they are a sceptical and conservative lot. Experimental evidence is there, and interest is growing.

Jane Carter was a schizophrenic – until wheat allergy was diagnosed. Symptoms can be profound and various; be assured, allergy can be more than hay fever and eczema. Bee-sting and penicillin allergy can kill, as can asthma, which often has an allergic component. Other allergies can make you more susceptible to serious disease in later life: Crohn's disease, ulcerative colitis and cancer of the small intestine have all been linked with allergy. If you yourself have symptoms which do not respond to ordinary medical treatment, consider allergy. **You have nothing to lose by trying**.

ALLERGY – DID YOU KNOW?

★ It is estimated that 35 million Americans suffer one allergy or another.

★ Coeliac disease, sensitivity to the gluten in wheat, was first explained by a Dutch doctor in World War II. He noticed that some children's health actually improved, despite famine conditions, because of the total absence of wheat in the diet.

★ At a world medical congress an American doctor reported success in treating baldness by withdrawing certain foods from patients' diets.

★ An Illinois farmer treated his severe allergic reaction to bee-sting with electric shocks. This treatment is now being used by doctors for snakebite, and may be extended to mosquito bites.

★ My son and I have both suffered from allergies: one to chocolate and the other to wheat and dairy products.

Action on allergy

A recent study by a group of doctors, done in collaboration with *Which?* magazine, has discredited a number of commercial allergy testing clinics. Specimens from a fish-sensitive woman were sent to the clinics – none diagnosed the allergy. The only effective method of diagnosing food allergy is the elimination diet, though it is time-consuming and tedious. You may have trouble locating a doctor up on all the latest research, and many doctors are frankly sceptical. Allergy clinics with a high reputation may be found at:

   Guy's Hospital, St Thomas Street, London SE1. 01–407–7600.

   Middlesex Hospital, Mortimer Street, London W1. 01–636–8333.

Give them a ring. If you live outside London, they may be able to direct you to a suitable clinic.

One very effective method of diagnosing food allergy is the elimination diet. You can put yourself, via your GP, in the hands of an allergologist. For three weeks you will eat nothing but, say, lamb, cauliflower, apples and pears. A 'suspect' food will then be added to your diet, then another until there is a reaction.

A punishing ordeal, but one which has often helped sufferers. Only try this under medical supervision.

During the test you may suffer a nutritional deficiency, such as lack of vitamin C or calcium. However, as the test doesn't go on long, this should not be a serious problem.

You are more likely to be allergic to a common food such as wheat, dairy products, pork, oranges or eggs – so 'challenge' with them first. (Caution: watch packaged foods for wheatflour, additives and colourings.)

Some diseases that are or may be influenced by food allergy:

Arthritis: You will have to be patient and wait for the joints to repair.

Asthma: Often linked with eczema. House-dust mites and mould are suspect.

Diabetes: A serious killer and crippler. If sugar, why not some other food?

Eczema: See asthma. Can be painful and embarrassing.

Migraine: Caused by chocolate, red wine, nuts etc.

Multiple sclerosis: Case not proven, but still under consideration.

Osteoporosis: A paradox: you need the calcium, but milk may make it worse.

27

HERBS AND SPICES
Variety in life and diet

It's difficult to know whether herbal medicines are good for you – unless you feel and believe they are.

Herbal medicine has been around for quite a while. *The Herbal of China* appeared about 3000 BC. Herbal doctors exist throughout the world among every kind of peoples. They must have done some good just to get us here.

It can be hard to distinguish between herbs and food, and food, of course, is good medicine. Is the onion a herb? How about parsley? Then again, we have the spices, essential ingredients of such healthy foods as vegetable curry. It should be said, at this point, that spicy food, if consumed in quantity over many years, can be dangerous, and it has been linked, among other diseases, to cancer of the oesophagus.

Generally speaking, though, herbs and spices, while they may

ALL THE SPICES OF ARABY

★ Vasco da Gama's trip to India, the first by boat from Europe, reaped a rich harvest of spices such as pepper. His cargo was sold for 60 times the cost of the trip on his return to Lisbon.

★ In 1977 a special type of ginseng was selling in Hong Kong for £10,000 an ounce. It was reputed to have aphrodisiac qualities.

★ The emperor Shen Nung is supposed to have invented herbal medicine in China (as well as the plough). In his researches with plants, he reputedly poisoned himself 80 times a day, but always recovered, as he was such a good doctor.

★ In herbal preparations, the Chinese have used cicada shell, seaweed, tangerine skin, dried yellow clay and donkey skin.

★ Green hellebore, from North America, was widely prescribed in the 1950s for lowering blood pressure. It went out of fashion with the development of chemical anti-hypertensives.

★ Wolfsbane, once used as a sedative and narcotic, got its name from its function as a poison bait for wolves.

---

not do you enormous good, are unlikely to cause much harm. And that's a lot more than can be said for some prescribed drugs of the recent past. Remember Thalidomide and Opren? Research has failed to unearth any fatal cases of nettle tea or pepper poisoning. Chillis can cause transient pain at either end of the alimentary canal, but little permanent damage has been recorded, except, perhaps, to people with previous intestinal problems.

One very important function of herbs and spices is flavour. Tasty food inspires us to eat, always a good move, though over-indulgence and obesity are perilous. There are economic benefits as well. A cheap, nutritious cut of meat (such as shin) may be made delicious with a pinch of this and that. For those on low incomes curry powder can be a godsend. It also helps camouflage high meat in hot climates.

There are endless claims for the medicinal uses of herbs. Russian herbologists, for instance, trust a concoction of vodka, pine needles and cones as a measure to prevent the onset of heart attack and stroke. Acacia is prescribed in Mexico for headache and indigestion. The Chinese swear by ginseng. People in New Guinea chew ginger to cure colds and sore throats. The Yoruba of Nigeria treat childhood convulsions with 'agbo tuto' – green tobacco leaves soaked in urine, and occasionally chased down with gin. Comfrey is said to heal wounds well, and other conditions too. However, it may be toxic if consumed to excess.

Herbal textbooks are numerous, and professional herbal healers not rare. The botanical world is extensive and accurate knowledge of herbs requires many years of study. There are organizations such as The National Institute of Medical Herbalists that examines and licenses practitioners. Refer to them for further information, if your appetite has been whetted.

Herb teas substitute nicely for those old standbys, tea and coffee (which are, of course, themselves plants). You can buy teas to wake you up; after-dinner teas; soporifics and many others of varied tastes and claimed efficacy. Certainly, both tea and coffee have been accused of having harmful effects on the circulatory, digestive and nervous systems. A hot cup of peppermint will do very nicely, thank you.

Honourable mention must be given here to the periwinkle, whose derivatives, vincristine and vinblastine, have been enthu-siastically adopted by the medical profession. They are import-ant anti-cancer drugs.

Forget not the foxglove – it provides the life-saving heart drug digitalis.

A last thought: all medicines are derived ultimately from some kind of natural substance. There may well be many useful treatments yet to be discovered in the fields and forests of the world.

VEGETARIANISM
A whole way of living

People become vegetarians for three reasons:

1 The moral and aesthetic distaste for conditions of animal husbandry and slaughter.
2 The health benefits of eliminating meat – and, in the case of vegans, dairy products and eggs.
3 Cost.

To deal with the points one by one: the moral distaste is understandable, considering the prevalence of factory farming; the health benefits are possible, but disputable; the cost of a vegetarian diet is certainly less. This last point alone, particularly for poorer people, and perhaps for the world at large, is a justification for fruit and vegetables. It is undoubtedly possible to live a long and healthy life without meat or fish, provided that you take extra care to eat *properly*.

There are certain nutrients you will take in abundance on a sensible vegetarian diet, such as vitamin C, and you will never lack for fibre. On the other hand, there are some you may have to think more carefully about. (Incidentally, don't think that

---

VEGETARIAN PEOPLE

★ Famous vegetarians include Paul and Linda McCartney, Nigel Hawthorne (of 'Yes Minister'), Hayley Mills, Gandhi, Bernard Shaw and Tolstoy.

★ There have been notable athletes who were strict vegetarians. Murray Rose won three swimming golds in the 1956 Olympics; William Pickering set a record for the cross-channel swim in the same year; and the current Mr Greater Manchester, Linford McFarquar, adheres to the faith.

★ During World War I, the Danes were forced to adopt a virtual 100 per cent vegetarian diet. During this food emergency, their death rate from non-infectious diseases fell by 34 per cent.

★ The durian is a fruit popular in India and South-East Asia. It is said to be peculiarly good for the sex life, which may be explained by the fact that it is fertilized by bats. Unfortunately, its corpse-like odour has discouraged airlines from importing it to Europe. Strong men have been brought near tears by its renowned pong.

just because you're a vegetarian you may not be allergic to some food or other. The common food allergies, to wheat, dairy products and oranges, for instance, may strike vegetarian and carnivore alike.)

The nutrients you are most likely to miss are:

Vitamin B12. This applies particularly to vegans. There is some B12 in dairy products, but not a lot. Deficiency causes nervous problems (often heralded by parasthesiae, tingling in the limbs) and psychiatric distress. Severe deficiency can cause the once fatal disease, pernicious anaemia. This is now easily treated with B12 shots. Play safe and take supplements.

Iron. Lack of this can also cause anaemia, though not so severe a form. Good vegetable sources of iron include: lentils, dried apricots, dates, kidney beans, fresh broccoli and prune juice.

Calcium. This deficiency will not much apply to milk drinkers and cheese munchers. Vegans can look to sesame seeds (and tahini, which is made from them), carrageen (Irish moss), kale, mustard greens, fortified soy milk and turnips, among others.

Zinc. In the last few years severe zinc deficiency, resulting in dwarfism and retarded sexual development, has been recognized in some parts of the Middle East. Also lack of zinc, or the inability to absorb it, has been suggested as a possible cause of anorexia. Zinc is particularly important for pregnant women. It is found in nuts and, especially, pumpkin seeds, available in most health stores. If in doubt, get supplements.

People often think that protein is a problem for vegetarians but this is rarely the case. The important thing is to get the right kind of plant proteins together on the same plate. Many poor cultures have devised the right balance of foods to provide adequate protein: beans and rice, for instance, or lentils and chapatis, or beans on toast. Remember that enforced vegetarianism, owing to straitened financial circumstances, has been the lot of much of mankind for many years.

In these days of plenty, vegetable puritanism makes no sense. Exotic plants are available from all over the world, so why not enjoy them? True, they cost a bit more than homegrown, but not that much. Too many vegetarians deny themselves the pleasures of yam, bitter gourd and jackfruit. Why spend one's life chewing carrots, when modern communications have brought such a cornucopia to the door? Many restaurants now offer vegetarian dishes, and many shops stock those little organic treats. As long as you're healthy, feel free to graze far and wide. And if a gardener, you'll be surprised how many unexpected and tasty varieties can be grown back in your own garden.

Yes, vegetarianism is here to stay. At the last count, there were 1½ million in Great Britain, many of whom will never touch meat again.

61

GARLIC
Handle with care

Soupe à l'ail
2 tbsp goose or other dripping
24 cloves garlic
2 litres (3–4 pints) warmed stock or water
salt, black pepper, mace and nutmeg to taste
3–4 egg yolks
3 tbsp olive oil
slices stale bread
4 egg whites

Put dripping into a deep earthenware casserole and melt the garlic cloves but do not allow them to brown.

Pour over them the warmed stock or water.

Season to taste and leave to simmer for 15 minutes.

Put the soup through a sieve, then return to pan and reheat.

In a bowl beat the egg yolks with the olive oil. Stir some of the hot soup into the beaten eggs, then pour egg mixture back into the soup without letting it come to the boil.

Dip the bread in the unbeaten egg whites and toast in the oven. Place toast in the bottom of soup plates and pour the hot soup over them. Serve immediately.

Whether this dish will do your health any good at all, who knows. Because garlic smells so powerful people get a veritable 'gut feeling' that it must be able to chase away invading germs; many a would-be guru has made it a pet treatment. We have yet to see experimental evidence that backs up these guesses with real proof.

It's tasteful, though, that must be admitted, and as for power, the garlic soup will certainly be effective in driving away enemies – or friends – who have not been lucky enough to share it with you.

PEARLS OF GARLIC

★ Aristophanes records that athletes would eat garlic before their exercises in the stadium.

★ In Cayenne garlic is used against bites of certain snakes.

★ Garlic has been used in the past as a cure for consumption, fever, epidemic diseases, intestinal worms and as a laxative and diuretic.

 **30**

PROTEIN
Needing it and getting it

For years, western notions about a healthy diet have centred on eating lots of protein, mainly in the form of meat. Now there is a fashion for saying that too much protein may be *bad* for us, particularly the protein found in meat. Yet we certainly need protein, in the right amount. Don't undersupply yourself.

What is protein? It is one of the six nutrients composing the food we eat. Proteins, in the plural, are the essential building blocks of human cells, made up of 22 amino acids. Eight of the 22 are called 'essential amino acids' (EAAs), because the body cannot manufacture them and they must come from the food we eat. As protein cannot be stored in the body, we should eat foods containing the eight EAAs *daily*.

Protein plays a great and varied role: it replaces and builds tissue, forms antibodies, aids digestion and regulates the body's water balance and basic metabolism. Some proteins are called hormones; others enzymes; an important one is haemoglobin, which carries oxygen via the blood to all cells.

We are around 12 per cent protein by weight: skin, hair, nails, cartilage, tendons, muscles, and even the outer bone layer consist of fibrous proteins. While carbohydrates, fats and protein all provide carbon, hydrogen and oxygen, *only* protein contains nitrogen, sulphur and phosphorus: substances essential to life. Protein also serves as a back-up energy supply if carbohydrate and fat reserves become exhausted.

How much protein is the 'right amount'? Our needs are largely defined by our body size, weight and activity rate. We need roughly one gram of protein daily for each kilogram of body weight. Protein should take up 12–15 per cent of daily calories – athletes may need up to three times this. Pregnant women, nursing mothers, the ill and the stressed, also need more.

DID YOU KNOW?

★ It takes 1.63 acres to feed a meat-eater, half an acre a vegetarian.

★ It takes 21 lb of plant protein to feed a cow to produce 1 lb of beef.

★ To gain extra muscle mass, protein alone won't do – you must weight-train too.

★ Soya-bean curd is closest to meat in protein value.

WAYS

31~40

THE DANGEROUS AGES

People die from different causes at different ages. Pneumonia is a major killer for babies and the very old, yet unimportant for those in their prime. Big differences show up between the sexes too . . . twice as many *boys* under ten get run over as girls – too macho? While among the over seventies, twice as many elderly *women* die of pneumonia as men.

See these dramatically different dangers for various age zones:

Under 1 year	cot deaths
1–4 years...	injury and poisoning
5–14 years	pedestrian deaths
15–24 years	motor cycles
25–34 years	suicide
35–44 years	heart disease
45–54 years	heart, cancer
55–64 years	lung cancer, heart
65 and over..	heart, lungs, cancer

For the very young it's the family that has to be forewarned. The parents must act to allow them the best chance in life. Yea, the actions of the parents are verily visited on the children . . . as with pregnant women and smoking.

Cot deaths, of infants under eight months, present a different problem, defying foresight, for doctors have not discovered the causes.

Where causes are known, it is often the remedies that are difficult to apply. How do you distract your son from desiring that lethal weapon, the motorcycle? Nevertheless in the ceaseless battle to keep every member of the human race alive and well, the world's ambition these days, we must go on trying to make life safer for such lads.

It's when a woman is young that she needs the exercise and the calcium in her diet (from milk) that will protect her against thinning bones when she's aged and it's too late to build them up. And brittle bones are a major cause of death in elderly women: see Way 40.

Watch for danger in *every* age band, so that you can act in time against the perils that cast their shadows before.

31

GENES AND HEREDITY
Choosing your parents wisely

From the beginning society has tried to control breeding. In fact, it may be that controlled breeding, ritualized in the careful mating process we call 'marriage', is one of the major factors in the remarkable progress of humankind. Incest has been banned throughout history, with extremely rare exceptions, such as the royal houses of the Egyptians and Incas. Small, 'primitive' tribes have complex systems of kinship – family relationships – which seem to exist to ensure that people marry as far away as possible from their close relatives.

Some scholars consider that marriage, and perhaps even society, evolved specifically to encourage outbreeding and ensure the birth of bonnie babes.

Considering genetic factors when marrying may seem un-romantic – but we all do it. As they say, opposites attract. The tall, dark type will often fall for the petite, fluffy blonde. Male professors are notoriously soft on foolish actresses, and female professors have often sought bliss with sweaty truck-drivers. It's only natural.

There are billions of people out there in the world to marry, and modern transport and communication has kept Love's flame a-burning from Giggleswick to Vladivostok. And why not? We're all a mixture of genes, good and bad, and the mixing will continue as long as the species does.

Having children can be a lottery, but now that modern scientific methods are available, it may well be possible to avoid tragedy and improve further the health of your offspring. Some screening is easily available, and doctors are trained in genetic counselling. If needed, ask for a consultation with a geneticist. By marrying wisely you may be able to avoid inflicting tragic congenital conditions on your children.

PASS THE GENES AROUND

Genes for talent or cleverness are passed on, not only genes for disease. The Swiss family Bernoulli produced six eminent mathematicians. J. S. Bach came from a long line of musicians and three of his sons, C.P.E., W.F. and J.C., are still important figures in the repertoire. In our own time the Huxleys are notable: Thomas, Julian, Aldous and Andrew have all had distinguished careers, particularly in the sciences.

32

COT DEATH
Be watchful!

On a December afternoon Maureen and her husband Rod tiptoed into their nine-week-old son Timothy's room, just for a peek. They found him not sleeping, but dead. It was the chilling cot death.

They caught Timothy up in their arms and drove quickly to the local hospital; Maureen rushed in clutching him close to her. Noting that the baby was not breathing, the staff bypassed the reception procedures, took little Timothy from Maureen and sat her down in a side room accompanied by a member of the staff. Alas, eventually the baby's death was confirmed by the hospital paediatrician.

Sudden infant death syndrome, or cot death, had claimed him, in that story related by Jacquelynn Luben, who lost her own seven-week-old Amanda the same way. Jacquelynn tells of another mother who looked in on her month-old babe one morning, pleased that the child had slept through the night. She was on her own at the time, except for her two small boys. When she discovered the baby, her screams attracted the attention of neighbours, who came to assist her. One, a nurse, tried mouth-to-mouth resuscitation and an ambulance was called. But there was nothing to be done.

The most common cause of death in children a few months old, cot death, was not known at all until recent years. Now it's clear that the incidence was always as high as today, perhaps 1500 a year. It simply wasn't recognized, because there were no signs to be noted before death, and none to be found afterwards. The anomaly remains that it still has no known cause, except for being the sum of a number of separate, mysterious causes.

There is just that common factor: the infant, happy and apparently healthy beforehand, is discovered cold and dead; and no apparent reason can be traced. The parents are left devastated, perhaps feeling guilty, never able to find out why the death occurred or what they might have been able to do to help.

But slowly science is closing in on certain possible causes. The latest suspect of research is upper respiratory tract infection set off by sudden, severe, winter weather. The bulk of deaths happen in winter.

The syndrome will be tackled in years to come, the cause or causes isolated and treatments will surely be found. Until then, because of the very nature of the problem, there is little we can do to guard against it. Except perhaps to keep babies in their first six months in the same room as the parents. Further than that the most we can do today is help the bereaved parents to cope.

WAR
Don't choose this way to die young

Probably the single most effective way to preserve our favourite species, Man, is to do away with war. The philosophers of medicine classify war, with little ceremony, as a macroplague, along with diseases like typhoid and smallpox. In the case of war it is other human tribes, not animal species such as rats and germs, that are the invaders spreading death.

We've managed to knock many spots off typhoid and to abolish smallpox altogether; now we need to cure ourselves of war. Not only would permanent peace save lives innumerable but, relieved from the duty of maintaining armies, the nations could devote huge budgets to life-enhancing activity.

No doubt war ministers and armament makers would sob sadly about the harm that would be done to 'defence', as they delicately call it, but the truth is the real damage would be to their own interests – such people would no longer need to exist. The fewer armaments in existence the less the need for defence; a practical example is the British policy of sending constables on to the streets unarmed, which has the result that gun battles are rare in crime war in Britain.

How can we stamp out war throughout our world? We will have to be very strong to win this battle, because the people of war are strong and they will expect us to fight to the death to defend their property. They are strong and they are aggressive, that's the very reason they're in that business of war in the first place. It's for every single individual to play a part in opposing them. Nor is it good enough just to take an anti-nuclear stance. Banning the bomb or for that matter chemical or biological warfare will simply force them back to conventional arms; tens of millions have been killed this century in conventional wars; even before gunpowder was invented scores of millions were killed by spears or swords or simple knobkerries.

As a first practical step let's vote for a Minister of Peace, to have at least equal seniority in the Cabinet with the Minister of War.

Younger people must also think out their own personal attitudes to a positive involvement in the war process, i.e. joining the forces. Speaking as one who voluntarily joined the Navy during the last war, I nevertheless would not take such a step today and I would advise any man or woman thinking of a service career: don't (as Mr Punch put it). That is certainly one way you will be putting your own lifespan at higher risk than normal. You will be in the front line against death.

Life is very precious and it is not replaceable. Do you consider it right for society to expect this sacrifice of you?

34

MOTOR BIKES
Easy there, rider

There are two sets of cowboys who give motor cycling its bad name. They are the out-and-out muggers, who show deliberate lack of consideration for others, and the 'serious' riders, who ignore danger and are happy to take risks on their own behalf (though this also may involve the downfall of others).

Both types are to be found in the ranks of the despatch riders, whose rate of earning depends on their speed in crossing town. These fellows can be seen wriggling through jammed rows of vans and cars, as likely as not on the wrong side of the white line, and hunting pedestrians along the pavements. Virtuoso performers they may be, yet they experience a high death rate – suicide rate it could be better called.

It's a difficult job to police and discipline these will-o'-the-wisp operators. The most the motoring organizations can do is appeal to their courtesy – well, good luck! There is more promise in the other campaign being pressed by the motor cycle industry, for legislation to make bike training compulsory. Unbelievably, the bike, this savage weapon aimed at the nation's youth, is on sale to any casual buyer, who may jump straight on a new machine and wobble off into the traffic, risking our lives as well as his, without training.

Nevertheless some progress is being made in looking after the safety of the million or more bike users. In the past ten years,

---

BIKING STATISTICS

★ In 1818 a steam-powered bicycle was run on the streets of Paris. It did not meet with much success.

★ The first motor cycle race was held over one mile at Richmond, on 29 November 1897.

★ The first motor cycle fatality happened in Vincennes, France, during a race in May 1899.

★ Every day two people are killed on motor bikes in Britain.

★ One fifth of all traffic accidents involve motor bikes.

★ In 1987 Duncan Baxter created a new world record, by balancing his stationary motor bike for 2½ hours, without his feet touching the ground.

What should be done

At 17 you can get a provisional licence, buy a 125cc machine capable of 70 mph, and ride it off without any training at all. Although most motor traders offer a training course, at present three-quarters of new learner riders opt to remain self-taught. The motor cycle industry, anxious to bring down the accident rate, is campaigning the government for the introduction of an obligatory 4-hour introductory training course, with lessons prior to the test.

though there are as many bikers as ever, their rate of accidents has dropped about 10 per cent.

They have been taught many things – for instance to keep their headlights switched on during the day so that they become visible to oncoming motorists and can be more easily avoided. (In some countries it is law for drivers of all vehicles to pursue this cheap and effective way of saving life.)

Another lesson was on how to use their brakes! It was discovered just lately, through brilliant application of accident statistics, that many bikers were crashing because they but used half their braking power – their back brakes only – in emergencies. Why were they so foolish? Because they remembered as youngsters on push cycles that you could topple over the handlebars if you applied the front wheel brakes hard. They thought they were being wise. However, the motor bike, being a far heavier apparatus than the push bike, the rear end stays solidly on the road when the front brakes go on – yet *more braking is needed* to reduce its forward momentum.

There is a different and additional reason for the current slowdown in the sales of bikes and consequently in the accident rate: there are fewer teenagers nowadays, due to smaller families in the 60s; birth control 20 years ago is assisting death control today in improving the statistical outlook.

But it's essential for government and public to put in an effort at slowing the death rate yet further – almost 1000 a year still, plus 100 pillion passengers, is too high a toll. More publicity and persuasion is needed, but that's not enough. It is absurd to leave control to the youthful rider alone. The moment he flings himself across a motor cycle for his first outing our teenage hero believes himself a wizard of the wheel and is anxious to show this off to others. He convinces himself at any rate that no harm can come to him. Yet as a beginner he is then at his most vulnerable, but so much in the grip of a macho mood that he cannot help himself. It is the responsibility of society to tie him down, until he learns discretion as well as skill.

UNEMPLOYMENT
Making a grand life of it

Unemployment is nothing new. It plagued Ancient Rome and, more recently, it brought Hitler to power. Undoubtedly it causes illness, not just for society but for the individual too. Suicide and depression are the visible tip of the iceberg – but underneath lies a large block of misery and chronic ill-health. Governments must deal with this problem: one of their prime functions is to ensure the good health of the population.

So much for wishful thinking. The fact is that there are several million in this country living on uncomfortably low incomes. Fretting and moaning will *not* improve their health, although concerted political action might well force government to re-direct resources and improve their economic status.

Lack of money is an obvious problem of the unemployed. This can result in inadequate food, clothing, housing, heating and entertainment – all of which are essential for good health. What can you do to feed the kitty? Casual work is a possibility – sometimes! It is also illegal if you earn more than a certain

---

LIFE-ENHANCING – MAYBE

★ In the spring of 1985, 45 per cent of the unemployed had been out of work for a year or more.

★ Unemployment's darkest black spot in Britain is Newquay, Cornwall. Of the 'working' population 27.4 per cent is on the dole.

★ In Germany, just prior to the accession of Hitler, there were 7,000,000 people unemployed.

★ A recent study shows younger unemployed dying at higher rates than the employed from suicide, other accidents, poisoning and violence.

★ Roosevelt's 'New Deal' in the 1930s succeeded in conquering the massive unemployment that followed the slump in the USA. The government invested in huge public works programmes, including the famed Tennessee Valley scheme.

★ It has been reported that as many as 60 per cent of all actors are unemployed, or 'resting', at any one time.

amount. Otherwise, it all comes down to *economy and improvisation*.

Aim high! Shop like an eagle and eat like a horse. The most important way to maintain your health on the dole is to **eat properly**. Don't resort to chips and beans. Good meat or fish should be taken every day – and if you're a vegetarian make sure you munch the very finest lentils. It is possible to eat three good meals a day on the dole, but it takes cunning and self-discipline. And don't rely on fatty meats like sausage and bacon. A nice bit of shin, well-curried, is as nutritious as steak. You might need to spend more time in the kitchen, but this can have its advantages. Good cooks are always popular.

There are other cottage crafts that can save money and improve your life. Make your own clothes, brew your own beer and wine, get an allotment. Think like a peasant, live like a lord.

Heating is often a problem. Underlay can be cheap, ditto curtain-lining. An electric blanket makes the bedroom more inviting, and pays for itself quite quickly. Roof and draught insulation grants are available from the authorities. Pressure your landlord to keep the house in trim, and if the council is your landlord, harass the councillors unforgivingly.

Cinemas run cheap shows, and many concerts and plays offer concessions to the unwaged. Always carry your UB40 and claim your rights. Some councils offer free entrance to sports centres –if yours doesn't, harass those councillors again. Libraries, of course, are free. Some even lend out records free – back to the councillors!

The loss of pride and identity associated with unemployment is less specific than the loss of income. Older men, particularly, find themselves at a loose end when out of a job. But there can be a lot of advantages gained from the free time. Many people have developed themselves in quite unexpected ways through the parsimonious courtesy of the DHSS. They have discovered music, painting, poetry, computers, sculpture, politics, woodwork and medicine. Even foreign travel. You may think it far-fetched, but unemployment has driven people to France for the grape harvest, Greece for the peaches, Spain for the oranges and just about everywhere for English language teaching. It's not so easy for those with families, of course – but children grow up fast.

Young Johnny Norris is a case in point. Like his father before him (and so on), he went into a factory. The factory closed, and he was on the Nat King Cole. With time on his hands, he turned his thoughts to jazz. Now, through study and involvement, he has become the best jazz pianist in Mugminster. And he's still on the dole! The moral is: he enjoys his life of music, even though professional jazz in Mugminster is not a possibility. He does earn the odd tenner every couple of weeks, if the wind is blowing in the right direction.

NO TO SUICIDE
Go for the good neighbour policy

Suicide ranks in the top ten causes of death, its weight falling most terribly of all on the young adult. So the statistics say; a still grimmer picture appears if one leafs over and over the figures – shouldn't the many who drink or drug or smoke themselves to death be also counted in the suicide class?

In Britain suicide is a disease that is growing rapidly, quite out of hand . . . it has commanded a rise by a quarter this last decade. And it is among the young adults that growth is fastest.

One can clearly see a tie-up between the disease and the social situation of our age, a fading national economy with high youth unemployment. People take their own lives because they believe they are not of use, not valued; then they simply write themselves off. Like some animals, when they surrender position in the pecking order they are ready to surrender life itself.

Those who have suffered a knock in their self-appreciation have to be given renewed confidence in themselves and in what they do, and that's a job for the community. They think themselves of no use to the community, but the community *needs*

TAKING THEIR LIVES IN THEIR HANDS

★ There is one suicide every two hours in Britain, every 20 minutes in the USA.

★ There is one suicide attempt every two minutes in Britain; principal methods are overdose, vehicle exhausts and hanging.

★ A family of five young Indian sisters hanged themselves from the same tree in Durban, South Africa.

★ The Samaritans receive 2,000,000 calls a year.

★ A half of those who kill themselves have seen their doctor in the previous fortnight.

★ Suicide is the second highest cause of death among young adults. Almost 90 per cent of the young who attempt suicide are females – yet males succeed more often, forming 70 per cent of the deaths.

★ It's merely a myth that lemmings leap to their death in huge numbers.

The 13 danger signs

(As drawn up by the Samaritans)

1 The person is withdrawn, cannot relate to you.
2 A family history of suicide.
3 Earlier attempts at suicide.
4 Definite idea of how suicide would be committed.
5 The tidying up of affairs, indicating suicide is being planned.
6 Anxious tone.
7 Dependence on alcohol and drugs.
8 Painful illness and long sleep disturbance.
9 Feeling of uselessness. In elderly, lack of acceptance of retirement.
10 Isolation, loneliness and uprooting.
11 Lack of a philosophy of life, such as religion or political belief.
12 Financial worries.
13 Within the period of the rise and fall in mood the most dangerous time is when the person appears better. Now he has enough energy to kill himself.

(The Samaritan system is clearly efficacious . . . a tiny proportion only of their callers take their lives.)

them, for, sentimentality aside, it cannot afford waste of its resources. The message is not only Love Thy Neighbour but help him to find some involvement in life, a worthwhile occupation at the least.

For yourself as an individual it is a Catch 22 situation: it is very difficult to give *yourself* a hand up. How do you even put yourself on guard against the taking of your own life? Because once you're on the nosedive path you may already be too ill to recognize the fact or do anything much about it. It's easier for those around you to help. And that is why in turn you must be particularly caring for your nearest relatives and your dearest friends, watching out for the tell-tale and dangerous signs.

There's an additional reason: by helping to save their lives, you're actually helping to save your own. For statistics tell us that the most dangerous situation to be plunged into is having a spouse commit suicide. The risk of suicide in the survivor, you, is increased 1000 times; and increases greatly also in the case of other relatives or close friends.

The principle is that you *are* your brother's keeper. Watch for danger signals that tell of emotional risk, so that you can rally help. For the other person's sake . . . and yours.

37

MURDER
Hold the front page

The ordinary citizen may breathe easily, in spite of newspaper efforts to drum up a modern horror tide of murder – your chances of being involved in a real life murder scenario are less than of winning the pools. (Hands up who's ever won a million.) For murder, though perhaps the most terrible death, is but a tiny item in mortality statistics. The fact that it's rarely off the front page is due to the papers seizing on almost every one of the few hundred cases a year.

What the media are doing is taking the spotlight off the real issues. Why not campaign against road accidents, where 5000 die a year?

FROM THE ARCHIVES

★ Men are arrested for murder roughly six times as often as women.

★ The greatest proportion of those murdered are in the 20 to 40 age group.

★ The majority of murders are committed with sharp instruments such as knives. Among women there is a high proportion also of deaths by hanging or strangling.

★ The New Orleans Axeman killed 8 people in the years 1918 and 1919, many of them Italian grocers. He was never caught.

★ Murder rates vary enormously around the world. According to Interpol, in one typical year:
   Lesotho had the highest rate of 140.81 per 100,000 (total of 1592).
   Norway had the lowest rate, 0.50 per 100,000 (total 20).
   The biggest single totals were in the USA (18,155) and India (19,480).
   The rate for England and Wales was 1.24 (total 602).
   The rate for Scotland was 3.82 (total 199).
   Only one person was murdered in Monaco.

★ Statistically speaking, the one person you are most likely to be murdered by is your spouse.

★ More than 50 per cent of white South African households possess guns.

Put 'em in the stocks!

That's what I'd do to these categories of people whose activities, leading to many mega-deaths, are in total effect no more than socially acceptable forms of murder:

    The pied-pipers who lead our young into taking up cigarettes.

    The pushers of drugs.

    The men and women who drink then drive, thus killing others.

    Those who send our sons to war or incite the nations to rage so furiously together.

    Those in government who deal negligently, apathetically, violently or viciously with the lives of the people.

    Those in the Press who keep the real issues obscured by sensationalizing murder, rape and violence . . . serving but to aggravate them.

A front page exclusive every day about these matters or a story attacking over-indulgence in alcohol or supporting the exercise movement would allow the media to show its concern and would save thousands of lives every year. Not so spicy?

The number of murders won't in any event be reduced by newspaper glamorizing, the reverse if anything, for the truth is that murder is the symptom of a sickness in individuals and in society, and needs deep and understanding treatment, not a lynching mentality with attendant publicity.

Furthermore most murders turn out to be family affairs, hardly susceptible to propaganda, whether they be crimes of passion, premeditated conspiracies concerned with property and wills, or spur-of-the-moment explosions of anger. This is even so in countries such as South Africa where there are many thousand murders a year – and where the State often adds its own contribution.

Whatever the problems that move people to kill their own family members they occur in greater proportion where there is poverty, educational backwardness, parental ignorance, mental feebleness. These are all signs of illness in society itself; the illness of not caring for the underprivileged.

Murder itself is not the danger. The danger is in dwelling on its ghastliness and glitter, while we let poverty and other social ills go unchecked, while we allow murder to be committed in the cause of war and while we let ourselves drift into a state of mind where we routinely accept murder's intrusion and its aggrandizement on our front pages.

OBESITY
Too many square meals

Get fat and die young. That is the simple message. Obesity undoubtedly increases your chances of a serious or fatal illness. In most cases obesity is easily treatable, at any age. But it requires a little self-control and willpower.

Fat people may often assume a humorous personality, and they are frequently the subject of cruel and thoughtless jokes. But death at 50 is no joke. Lose unnecessary fat, and you will live longer. You will also be less susceptible to a whole range of crippling and painful diseases: diabetes, arthritis, gallstones, bowel cancer, varicose veins and piles, to mention a few.

There are a few people with hormonal or other abnormalities that cause obesity. But the vast majority are obese because they:

1 Eat too much.
2 Exercise too little.

These are the bald facts.

Obesity is a social disease – it is common in affluent countries such as the USA and UK, and rare in poor countries. Curiously, it is more common among the poorer classes of the developed countries (where food is cheap compared to income), and at the same time more common among the upper classes in the underdeveloped countries. Slenderness is a mark of social status in the USA, while the opposite is true in India.

Quite often obese people do not eat much more than their slender friends and relatives. The reason for this is simple: they use up less energy in the normal, everyday practices, such as

---

FAT FACTS

★ It has been estimated that life expectancy diminishes by two per cent for every kilo of body weight above normal.

★ The current world weight record is that of Jon Brower Minnoch – he reached 100 stone, but on a diet went down to 34 stone.

★ There are suggestions that obesity and diabetes may be causally linked. The theory states that the body produces *too much* insulin, and this excess upsets the mechanisms for controlling blood sugar.

★ It has been estimated that at one time in the 1970s 50 per cent of American women were overweight.

Ways to lose weight

★*Exercise*. If too self-conscious to run or swim in public, you could do much worse than invest in an exercise bike. These can be easily stored in a cupboard. Kids and friends will make use of them too. T'ai chi and dance can be practised in private and are effective. But exercise must be done daily.

★*Psychotherapy*. Obese people are often hypersensitive, passive types. They eat when under stress, as a reward or compensation. Food can be a substitute for love. As with other addictions, psychotherapy can be of benefit. Weight watchers are basically a therapy group.

★*Acupuncture and hypnotism*. As for the above, these are often helpful in combating addiction, and helping the patient to learn to take control of his or her own life.

★*Drugs*. These are a last resort, but should be considered for 'hopeless' cases. As obesity can be so dangerous, particularly for types II and III, drugs should never be ruled out.

sitting, standing and walking. Food intake has to be related to energy output. Just one unheeded slice of bread a day can build up, over ten years, to an extra 20 kilos of fat deposited. This is no problem for the person who burns it off. But for those with a tendency towards obesity, it can be fatal. The problems of energy expenditure and food consumption last for life. Children often eat large amounts, but do not become fat. The reason is that they run around all the time, causing havoc to parents and teachers alike. If you are obese, think and act like a child, and your health and life expectancy will improve dramatically.

On the other hand, plumpness is not a serious problem. The scientific measurement of obesity is complex, and you should consult your doctor for an accurate diagnosis. There are three grades recognized, I, II and III. If you are II or III, you really should start worrying. Body weight alone is not an accurate measurement. If you are in any doubt, consult an expert.

It is quite possible to lose 20 kg of weight in 20 weeks. The number of diets available are numerous, but they all depend on the patient's perseverance. Because of the difficulty obese people have in holding on to the desire to lose weight, it may be of benefit to supplement diet with other techniques.

In general, your best bet is to carry on eating normally, but cut down on quantity. If you exercise enough, you may even find that you can eat as much as you want. Sugar should be avoided, but only because it gives no feeling of fullness, and probably increases the appetite, and it's very tempting to lash out on some sweet item instead. Use beer money for buying salmon.

RETIREMENT
Roads to freedom

Retirement is a reward. After 40 or 50 years' work you are free to do whatever you like. Unfortunately the rewards do not always turn out so great. The state pension doesn't go too far, and not everybody has the benefits of a private scheme. But then again, there's never enough money about.

The first thing to do of course is take care of your health – all those constant little details such as good food, exercise and the development of creative relationships with your doctor, social worker, family and friends. But by retirement, you should be old enough to know these things. The major task is to make use of those 35 years (or more!) that stretch out before you.

Have you heard the one about the psychiatrist who became a Cordon Bleu chef? Or the furniture salesman who took up acupuncture? Or the housewife who graduated in Spanish? Or the plumber who broke a world record in the high jump? All these characters are retired; and all they have in common is that they took the plunge into new ways of living. There's nothing stopping you, too, from discovering new aspects to your personality, new skills and new interests.

Let us here insert the tale of Duncan Maclean, 'The Tartan Flash'. Duncan lived an adventurous sort of life, fighting for the British and Germans in Africa, and for the British *against* the

---

ACHIEVEMENTS AFTER THE AGE OF 65

★ Churchill won the Second World War, with a little help from his friends Joseph Stalin and Franklin D. Roosevelt.

★ Verdi wrote *Falstaff* and *Otello*.

★ Clive Davies did the marathon in 3 hours 5 minutes at the age of 70.

★ Somerset Maugham published *A Writer's Notebook*.

★ Michaelangelo designed the dome of St Peter's.

★ Grandma Moses began her famous painting career at over 70.

★ Akira Kurosawa directed *Derzu Uzala*, *Kagemusha* and *Ran*.

Germans in the First World War. He achieved a modest fame as a music-hall entertainer and joined ENSA in the Second World War. Music hall and club work declined, so he slipped into painting and decorating. At 80 he retired and turned seriously to his favourite hobby, athletics. Once again fame blossomed as the Veterans' Athletics movement germinated. His inspired performances in the Super-Vet category won him medals, free trips abroad and widespread affection. Early in his nineties he nipped out of retirement to a pleasant little earner tidying up the Crystal Palace athletics track. And then, at 93, he retired. Shortly after, he died. Perhaps he shouldn't have retired so soon!

The moral of Duncan's story is that old age can be just as much fun as any other time of life. It may be a new beginning, another open door. Some may prefer the pleasures of contemplation, but, for such as Duncan, activity is the key. Remember, it's your freedom (within the economic parameters) to decide how to spend your time when you abandon the old 9 to 5.

Early retirement is often a possibility. Gauguin the painter set a precedent for this at 37 when he escaped from Paris to Tahiti. It makes sense, in our society of increasing automation and unemployment, for a man of 60 to try for a second career, and leave his job open to a 20-year-old. Women, of course, *can* retire at 60 – rather unfair when you consider that they live longer.

Keep active, you need the involvement – that's the message. Peter King retired as a printer in his fifties . . . during the next years he became chairman of the London Gliding Club and flew his glider all over Britain and Europe; he bought a motor-bike and rode right around the world to call on his ten children; he entered competitive marathon races; he twice walked the slopes of the Himalayas, pedal-cycled through many countries, took up weight-training, and became part-time treasurer of an important city guild. That's keeping going! That's involvement!

Those without involvement, who slump down without effort – 'ole rockin' chair will get them.

Some suggestions: new technology looks to be an interesting area for retirement entertainment or a second career. It is said that older people and children take to computers more easily than the rest of us! Perhaps this is because of the importance of the powers of *play*. Computers are not ashamed of being used as toys. Just tell a computer what to do, and it'll do it, if it can. Maybe the government should issue computers along with pension books. Who knows what marvellous inventions might emerge from the fertile minds of our senior citizens?

College courses abound, and local authorities and firms often run pre-retirement courses. University is definitely on if you get the required A-levels. Some old people have gained admission to university *without* qualifications. Shop around.

If the worst comes to the worst . . . write a book.

OLD BONES
Falls kill and disable – simple precautions

Falling is a common cause of death, a major cause in the home. In grown men and women there are actually as many deaths from falls as there are from road accidents. Yet traffic peril attracts the greater public to-do; equivalent attention given to precautions against falling would save many lives. And while fire brigades howl through the streets and onerous regulations are imposed on buildings, five times as many people are dying from simple domestic and industrial falls. The same money and dramatics spent on eliminating the causes of falls could whittle down the numbers invalided or killed.

Be warned yourself. Stay away not just from banana skins but from uneven pavements and oily patches in the workplace. Take care when doing-it-yourself up a ladder: see that it is strongly built and firmly propped, and if possible supported by an assistant do-it-yourselfer. Fit non-slip cups on the feet and head of the ladder. Asbestos roofs: real death traps these, they look safe yet are incapable of bearing an adult's weight; and you fall directly through to the concrete.

By far the largest proportion of fatalities from falls come among older people. Young children can safely bounce up and down but past retiring age a fall may lead to death within a year for many, particularly women. The most notable contributory

---

FROM A GREAT HEIGHT

★ Flying over Germany in March 1944, an airman, Nicholas Alkemade, fell out of his American bomber from a height of 18,000 ft, landed on a fir tree, bounced on to a snowbank and walked away with no bones broken.

★ Of all fatal accidents in the home 60 per cent are due to falls.

★ Of these fatal home accidents one-third are falls in the over 75s.

★ More than half of those who are medically classified as 'long liers', ie: remain lying for an hour or longer after a fall, die within six months.

★ A great proportion of falls leading to death occur among patients in hospital.

Fancy footwork for staying upright

★ Avoid excessive drinking – alcohol not only causes unsteadiness but actually contributes to brittleness in ageing bones.

★ Keep a lively attitude to life – mental and physical exercise, sex and waking earlier.

★ Spend money wisely on shoes. Don't trip yourself up through false economy. Avoid flip-flop slippers and high heels.

★ Treat your feet to extra care, including a yearly visit to a chiropodist.

★ Replace slippery rugs with rubber-backed mats.

★ If you fall and can't raise yourself or get immediate help, wiggle your toes, at the least. This, deep breathing, will keep circulation going and gradually help you to recover from the shock of the fall.

cause in these women is thin and brittle bones: a serious fracture means a greater chance of being confined to bed . . . and thus pneumonia gets its opportunity.

The time for a woman to start avoiding thin bones and osteoporosis is earlier in life. Regular exercise, milk when young and a good diet keep the bones dense and strong. Otherwise rate of bone loss can be as much as 1 per cent a year after the fifties, with the onset of the menopause. Here's what to do about it: take calcium enriched foods, get up earlier (thinning of bones occurs mostly while you're in bed!) and stimulate your adrenal glands by an active mental and physical life (exercise, excitement and sex), essential to help produce oestrogen.

An important way to avoid falls is to keep the body supple and the joints mobile. So keep fit through exercise. At least practise balancing daily. Stand on one leg (near a wall, for safety) and concentrate on balance, thinking into the action of your muscles. Ballet dancers do it.

Carry a stick when out and about.

Look after your feet. Massage, footbaths and toe-wriggling improve the circulation. A visit to that unsung hero, the chiropodist, at least once a year is recommended. Keep a watch out for trailing flexes and crawling grandchildren.

Finally, falls can be a sign or symptom of some underlying condition. If you do fall once, make sure to see your doctor for a check-up. Treatment will lessen your chances of another, perhaps more serious, fall.

WAYS
41~50
CRIPPLING ILLNESSES

Sometimes, for no understood reason, a person is struck down by one of the crippling diseases and never recovers completely. Such a one was the great young cellist, Jacqueline du Pré, a victim of Multiple Sclerosis.

One may die of MS, though many like Jacqueline survive, perhaps to full old age. But even if their time is not actually shortened they *are* robbed of an active, ordinary life.

The monetary, not only the human, cost is high too. Here's an estimate: a person with an income of £15,000 a year might normally expect to pull in as much as £1,000,000 in a lifetime, taking into account interest. That could be totally lost to a victim . . . add the cost of care, maybe as much again.

Official calculations of the cost to the community, sometimes taking into account pain, grief and suffering, show similar levels of loss. Scales of benefit awards are of that order, and, in cases where blame *can* be attached, so are court settlements.

Soon enough victims are going to try to pin down the blame, when medical science pins down the causes, and they will then be pressing for large compensation. For instance, it has become known in past years that Buerger's disease, a most painful condition, only attacks and incapacitates smokers. Slowly alcohol is coming under suspicion too for certain crippling diseases.

Radiation, asbestosis and industrial hazards, and accidents from fires, falls and traffic contribute to the pool of those with crippled lives. Government estimates of the annual cost of injuries are at the multi-billion pound level.

The note of hope is that year by year those hurt by accident will be more effectively repaired and that the crippling diseases, too, are sure to be tackled. Even people with Alzheimer's disease and MS may yet have their suffering alleviated; certainly there is optimism that for conditions like diabetes and arthritis help is less than a generation away.

41

THE GUT
CIBD and bowel cancer

Chronic inflammatory bowel disease is a term that covers two complaints: Crohn's disease and ulcerative colitis. (Bowel cancer is separate from these two.)

These are serious illnesses. Patients often require major surgery: colostomy and its sister, ileostomy. What's more, ulcerative colitis predisposes you to cancer of the bowel, and Crohn's may increase other cancer risks. CIBD is likely to become a battlefield in modern medicine. On the one side are conventional gastro-enterologists who advocate drugs and surgery. On the other are the clinical ecologists, who suggest that diet and other factors in our environment are the key.

Conventional medicine does not know the cause of these illnesses. However some studies indicate that diet may play a part in causation. A group at Addenbrooke's Hospital, Cambridge, is working on the problem.

Whatever the cause of CIBD the patient's main aim is survival without the onset of fatal disease. And of course a comfortable survival, without recourse to heavy drug use and surgery. Most people would rather adopt some 'strict' dietary regime than spend their lives coping with a bag of faeces, which is what the operations result in. But if the worst comes to the worst surgery is the only option; the bag is preferable to the grave.

Among the complications of Crohn's disease is arthritis, usually of a single large joint. There is also a high incidence of gallstones and kidney stones.

The disease is unfortunately not on its way out; in fact its incidence is said to have increased five-fold within the last 15 years. Some authorities have ascribed this to environmental pollution.

Cancer of the colon

The fibre fad first flourished when it was touted as possible protection against bowel cancer. Africans develop much less of this cancer than Europeans: is their fibrous diet the reason?

But there could be other factors at play: high intakes of vitamin C and potassium from fruit, for instance. Then again most Africans are not sedentary and must work hard to eat. Cancerous Westerners, on the other hand, classically overeat and underexercise – a recipe for disaster!

42

MULTIPLE SCLEROSIS
Hope at last

Life is looking brighter for MS patients. While one shouldn't expect miracles, there is now firm evidence that the disease can be stabilized. What was once feared as a condition that declined irreversibly is now a candidate for positive improvement.

Action for Research into Multiple Sclerosis (ARMS) recommends four methods of treatment. Patients may try all four, or settle for a suitable mix. They are:

1 The ARMS diet. This is basically a low fat, nutritionally complete diet, with an emphasis on fish, plus plenty of vitamin C and half a pound of liver a week.

2 Hyperbaric oxygen. Patients are fed oxygen under pressure in a special chamber. There are a number of these chambers around the country.

3 Physiotherapy. A rational programme of exercises, regularly undertaken, is of undoubted benefit.

4 Counselling. Patients and their families often suffer severe emotional problems, which can be much alleviated by professional counselling.

For further details, get your doctor to contact ARMS.

Multiple sclerosis occurs when the fatty, sheath-like covering of nerves in the brain and spinal cord are damaged. These

---

FACTS ON MS

★ There are 75,000 MS patients in Britain. The condition particularly favours young adults. Three well-known sufferers are the model Vivien Neves, and musicians Jacqueline du Pré and Ronnie Lane.

★ The Orkney and Shetland Islands have the world's highest incidence of MS.

★ MS has an odd pattern of attack and remission. The time between the first and second attacks may be as long as 25 years.

★ One study of a group of selected patients has shown that half of them survived for 35 years or more after the onset of the disease.

★ Visual and movement symptoms are the most common first signs of MS. 70 per cent of patients have nystagmus – involuntary side-to-side movement of the eyes.

Rules for MS patients

★ Avoid sudden and extreme changes of temperature, which seem to worsen the condition. Relapses commonly occur in winter and spring – times when movement from hot to cold environments are more likely. Wrap up warm, but stay cool.

★ Stick religiously to your diet. Remember, it may take some time for the beneficial effects of a sensible diet to become apparent, so persist with the fish, fruit and vegetables.

★ Take regular, gradual and gentle exercise. Don't build up your exercise regime too quickly. Consult a physiotherapist frequently.

★ Seek some kind of psychotherapeutic help.

sheaths are made of a substance called myelin. Nobody knows why the myelin breaks down, though theories abound: viruses, stress, diet and malfunction of the immune system have all been blamed. It is generally accepted that the immune system for some reason *is* at fault, because white blood cells are found infiltrating the brain and cord. MS is more common in cold climates, and it is thought the stressful conditions of such climates may trigger the degeneration.

Other therapies have been suggested, and may be useful, but as yet there is no convincing proof of their efficacy. These include clinical ecology (the avoidance of allergenic substances in some foods), homeopathy, more intensive counselling and psychotherapy and, of course, conventional drugs. Most patients survive for many years, and on occasions their improvement can be dramatic. One of the great problems is convincing patients that they *can* get better. Damage to the brain, and interference with basic functions, such as movement and bladder control, often cause great depression in the patient and consequent distress in friends and relatives. It is of primary importance to realize that years of research seem now to be bearing fruit. A positive attitude is the only way forward.

There are signs that MS patients are beginning to stand up for their rights. ARMS is trying hard to educate sufferers and the public at large. Many sufferers continue to work, travel, marry and have families. Of course, not all can manage these things, but the pioneers are striking out. The will to survive and thrive may yet consign the suffering to history.

43

PHOBIAS
Dealing with unreasonable fears

Fear and anxiety are normal human emotions, a certain degree of them being necessary for survival. Babies are born with an instinctive fear of loud noises (not only a capacity for producing them!) and little children know to stay away from the edge of a drop. Fears are often innate, but mostly learned.

Many people are afraid of, say, flying, closed-in spaces, heights, maybe spiders . . . yet they manage to lead normal lives. It's when such a fear becomes intense, persistent and unreasonable that it becomes a phobia. The phobic may or may not be able to avoid his phobia in everyday life; if he can't, it could seriously disrupt his life. He may have a deathly fear of dogs, which could prevent him leaving his house.

Anything can become the object of a phobia, but the most common falls under the category of **agoraphobia** (from *agora*, Greek for marketplace), a fear of open spaces. Other common phobias are closed spaces, being home alone, leaving home, and travelling on any form of transportation.

Phobias can be heralded by stress, illness or a single traumatic incident, but often come out of the blue. More feared than the feared object itself is the 'anxiety attack' phobia often brings about. It can include palpitations, nausea, trembling, sweating or shivering and is threatening not only for being

---

PHOBIC FACTS

★ Phobias are the second most common anxiety complaint treated.

★ 'Anxious' people are more prone to developing phobias because they 'condition' faster.

★ Introverts are also thought to be more susceptible.

★ Alcohol abusers have a particularly high rate of phobia: in one study of a group of alcoholics, two-thirds gave a history of agoraphobia.

★ Some medical conditions predispose to phobia, including PMT (pre-menstrual tension), over-active thyroid, and a tumour in the adrenal gland.

★ Fear of animals is more common among women, fear of illness among men.

What you can do

Use a prop – an umbrella, walking stick, shopping trolley, any reading material; even a dog can give added confidence.
Distract yourself – start a conversation with someone, or carry around a small card on which is written favourite memories or anecdotes (concentrate on them one at a time).
Take it slowly – if actually caught in an anxiety attack, remember to take it slowly. If you hurry, the attack will be worse. Take in your surroundings in great detail to help you forget your own state.
Self-help – the Phobics Society, a national charity, can be contacted at: 4 Cheltenham Road, Chorlton-cum-Hardy, Manchester.

unpleasant, but because it signifies a loss of control. Beneath every phobic fear is that bigger fear of losing control.

What can be done? Phobics need to realize that they can be in control, and that what has been learned, the phobia, can be *un*learned. First you should lessen anxiety by relaxing body and mind – through teaching yourself a relaxation technique, and carrying it out faithfully twice a day for ten minutes in a quiet room until total relaxation is achieved. Relaxation technique is about alternately tensing and relaxing each muscle group in the body, while inhaling and exhaling slowly, taking about eight minutes. Then spend a couple of minutes concentrating on a soothing mental image.

When relaxation has been achieved, introduce the phobia by degrees into your thoughts. If you are afraid of cats imagine yourself seeing one several feet away. Note which muscle groups have tensed up and concentrate on relaxing them. Then move on to the next stage, the cat a bit closer. Ultimately, you should be able to imagine your worst fear – the cat is sitting on you – while staying physically relaxed.

Ideally, carry this over into reality, using a process known as 'systematic desensitization'. If you are afraid of crowded supermarkets, start by just walking past the store, then move on to stepping inside the doorway, then visiting a part of the store nearest the exit when it's quiet, etc.

If you can't do this, you may want to work through the phobia with a therapist. The success of therapy is dependent not only on determination and discipline, but on the attitudes of family and friends. Some husbands do not like it when once-dependent spouses start to gain more confidence and a degree of independence! Phobics themselves may find it hard to give up being the centre of attention.

44

ARTHRITIS AND GOUT
Chronic pain and stiffness

Arthritis does not kill, but it shortens life – the constant pain undermines health and the will to live. Through the centuries the condition has yielded a myriad of treatments but no cures.

It was only in the nineteenth century that gout was classified as a distinct form of arthritis. Today arthritis is divided into many categories, the two most common being rheumatoid arthritis and osteoarthrosis: RA and OA.

Gout, RA and OA have different causes and affect different people. RA attacks three times as many women as men. Gout is largely man's prerogative. OA is mostly a disease of later life,

JOINT ANGULARITIES

★ There are an estimated 500,000 RA sufferers in Britain.

★ Rural Africans have a lower incidence of RA than urban Africans of the same genetic stock. This indicates a non-genetic, environmental factor in its cause.

★ There are more than 100 separate joint diseases in the modern classification.

★ Gout can be caused by lead poisoning.

★ Physical exercise was regarded as the reason for the low incidence of gout in Glasgow in 1814 – most of the population walked, there being only five cabs and 20 private vehicles in the whole city.

★ *Pithecanthropus erectus*, 'Java Man', who flourished 500,000 years ago, is reported to have suffered from OA.

★ Treatments for gout and arthritis in the past have included: leeches; ox-dung wrapped in cabbage leaf; roast goose stuffed with chopped kittens, lard, incense, wax and rye-flour; honey enemas; rhubarb; and the wearing of dog-skin stockings.

★ Colchicine has been used in the treatment of gout and arthritis for more than 2000 years.

★ The Roman physician Scribonius Largus treated arthritis patients with the torpedo fish, an electric ray. He placed the patient's feet on the fish: when the tide came in an electric shock resulted.

the cause being wear-and-tear.

Though no cures have yet been found, there are some successful treatments available. Hip replacement surgery is not to be sneezed at, but it doesn't help the crippled hand. Drugs certainly soothe in the short term, though some doctors argue that they can worsen the condition in the long run. The alternative therapists have offered no convincing proofs of their abilities to help, except in the case of the green-lipped mussel of New Zealand, where scientists have confirmed that it is efficacious for some people.

Help often comes down to common sense and individual responsibility as possible 'cures'.

1 Our old friend Exercise. Physicians since Hippocrates have prescribed it. Soranus of Ephesus (second century AD) noted that desertion of an active life could lead to joint disease. Try swimming, where the joints are gently worked.

2 Our other old friend Diet. Indulgence is undoubtedly a cause of gout. It may be true, too, of RA and OA. Clinical ecologists have reported significant improvement in patients who have excluded certain foods from their diets. Don't expect immediate results; you can imagine that bone needs some time to repair.

3 Our old enemy Stress. Once again doctors through the ages have seen links between stress and the onset of joint conditions. Try rest, massage and relaxation. Plan your campaign against stress when not in a stressed state and lay down rules to observe. When you are actually under stress is just the moment when it is difficult to act in a sensible, relaxed way.

4 Work things out for yourself. Jack may prefer judo, but finds milk damaging. Judy likes the Alexander technique (a system of postural re-arrangement), but can't take cake. With patience and logic, you may be able to help yourself to health.

Gout and rheumatism figure often on the stage of history. Among the distinguished cast were the Holy Roman Emperor Charles V, Lord Burghley, Elizabeth I's chief minister, both Pitts, Columbus, Mary Queen of Scots (in her neck, among other joints), Oliver Cromwell, George IV, Michelangelo, Luther, John Milton, Francis Bacon, Dr Johnson (not surprisingly!), Queen Anne and the great medic William Harvey.

Another medic of modern times, Christiaan Barnard, had been an RA sufferer ten years before his first epochal heart transplant operation. Unfortunately he has had to give up surgery now, but continues to write, teach and research. Art Blakey is perhaps the most admired modern jazz drummer. Aged 70, he suffers badly from arthritis, yet continues to lead a band of musicians young enough to be his children and grandchildren. The moment he hits the bandstand the outward signs of his condition disappear.

45

ALZHEIMER'S DISEASE
Help and hope for the carers

This is for those who care for victims of Alzheimer's disease, rather than for the victims themselves, for once they're in its grip they are no longer able, mentally, to take advantage of any advice. Nor is there a cure for this degeneration of the brain cells, a form of senile dementia.

The carers, on the other hand, need all the help and advice they can get, for theirs can be a difficult and distressing duty. Their charges not only have declining ability to remember, barely managing their day-to-day life, but they may behave quite uncontrollably. Outbursts of tears, spitefulness and aggression are among their catastrophic reactions to stress. They may become wanderers and become a danger to themselves. For some, death is an early release.

Here's what the daughter of one sufferer said: 'It's the mental strain . . . she hasn't any patience, she says unkind things. It's an unbelievable strain – you have to take it a day at a time.'

And the wife of a 58-year-old: 'Unable to socialize, read, write, give love or receive it, he's yet in need of the utmost tender care. Unable to walk, unable to talk . . .'

In fact the work of the official organization, the Alzheimer's Disease Society, is essentially to spread mutual help and understanding among the caring thousands – for there are as many as 750,000 victims of the disease in Britain alone.

The society also helps to promote research into treatment. Research of course continues worldwide and only lately has there been received a message of cautious hope from the USA. Controlled trials with a complex biochemical has shown some symptomatic benefit to Alzheimer patients. Those in the early stages who took a medicine that stimulates production of one of the major chemicals of the brain experienced some restoration of their memory and elimination of feelings of disorientation.

The very diagnosis of Alzheimer's is difficult and uncertain. Loss of recent memory is one of the insidious signs, but that is anyway an acceptable effect of ordinary ageing. Nor are blood supply problems in the brain, such as a series of small strokes, any longer thought to be normally connected with it. There are no simple tests of the condition and the GP may need to get a second opinion from a specialist. Finally only a post-mortem examination can bring absolute certainty.

Thankfully this lack of knowledge of the identity of the disease extends to the patient, who is usually unaware of it even when others can settle for a diagnosis. It is all the more necessary for relatives to understand the nature of the disease and its symptoms when planning to cope with the stress that will be

Practical steps

At the recognition of Alzheimer's disease relatives of the sufferer should discuss with solicitors joint financial affairs, wills, and the need to obtain a Power of Attorney or Court of Protection order.

All sufferers from AD should be registered with their local authority as disabled. They then qualify for higher rent and rate rebates.

Management strategies for the carer:

★ Good communication is important. Check hearing aids, glasses, dentures are working.

★ Speak clearly and simply, use body language to help communicate.

★ Draw patient's attention to memory aids such as clocks, calendars, room signs.

★ Deal with repeated questions with tact, tell the sufferer what is going on.

★ When speaking distinguish clearly between past and present.

Health and safety for carer and patient:

★ Check house for hazards: trailing wires, loose rugs. Keep medicines, domestic fluids, bleach etc. out of reach.

★ Supervise consumption of medicine and drugs and keep locked away.

★ Don't keep the problem a secret. Tell those close to you.

★ Take time off from caring. Enlist help of friends and relatives.

★ 'Switch off' at home when you are unable to cope. Ensure you have short spells of privacy to read, sit alone and relax.

★ Accept when you can no longer cope and consider full-time medical care for the patient.

created in their own lives.

These relatives may experience a sense of loss, even a sense of guilt, as well as anger and frustration, both with the patient and with professionals because they cannot offer adequate help. That's when they themselves need support both from the society and from local groups.

46
DEPRESSION
Halt the downward spiral

Depressed? If you have got this far you can't be too bad – a depressive finds it hard enough to summon up motivation for the next 24 hours let alone 99 years.

Slightly depressed? Most people feel temporarily 'down' at times. Take a good look at your life and see if some improvements are necessary. Does your day include any physical exercise? Are you piling too much work into your schedule? Or too little? Sometimes a walk, a change, a treat or a talk over a problem with the people concerned will do the trick. Try to analyse your position in terms of what could be done.

Very depressed? (This is still not major depression – a massive loss of interest in the outside world and where daily life has broken down. Immediate professional help is obviously essential.) The sense of deep hopelessness seems permanent; a grey feeling accompanies withdrawal from other people. Trivial activities seem impossibly difficult; pleasures fail; suicide can beckon.

For most depressives 'I *feel* hopeless' means 'I *am* hopeless'. Self-blame, self-pity rush in, guilt and inertia intensify.

Put a brake on this downward spiral – the sooner the better:

1 Recognize that you are depressed   It is amazing how often it goes unnoticed. The prolonged change of mood seems 'normal'. You think yourself 'weak' and cover up. Label the depression as something separate from yourself.

2 Ask why?   Depression is a symptom with many causes and

UPS AND DOWNS

★ John Bunyan was depressed for 30 years and wrote *Pilgrim's Progress* on the strength of it.

★ Winston Churchill warded off his 'black dog' with painting and bricklaying.

★ Among the complicated physical changes in the brain during aerobic exercise are the release of the depression-lifting, pain-blocking endorphins (run out and get some!).

★ 'The cure of this ill is not to sit still,
    Or frowst with a book by the fire;
  But to take a large hoe and a shovel also,
    And dig till you gently perspire.'
  (Rudyard Kipling: 'The Camel's Hump', *Just So Stories*)

Keeping going

Keep moving – find, with help a regular pattern of exercise.
Keep in contact with other people – interest groups, sport, congregations – even if it has to be fairly impersonal at first.
Keep feelings and actions separate.
Keep away, while severely depressed, from other depressed people.
Keep up hope – you won't *feel* hopeful but you can force yourself to *know* that you will pull through in the end.

can affect anyone. Here are some examples.

External causes. Loss is the greatest cause of pain, whether of a loved one, a familiar place, work companionship, physical ability, status, etc.

Physical causes. Viral infection, eg: flu; hormonal imbalance such as postnatal blues, PMT (pre-menstrual tension), adolescence; chemical imbalance caused by certain drugs and alcohol; possible hereditary tendency.

Personality causes. People who demand unreasonably high standards from themselves are likely to be beset with a sense of failure. Perfection seems normal, unobtainable only through their own worthlessness. People who are 'trapped' in doormat or dependent roles will be likely to endure recurring depression.

Perhaps you didn't recognize yourself in the list. Depression will often cloud self-perception to such an extent that no cause is seen except personal worthlessness.

3 Action Go to see a doctor. This may take quite an effort. Ignore internal voices telling you not to be a bother. When you get there it is helpful to you and the doctor if, as well as saying you are 'depressed', you describe some of the behaviour that is worrying you: lethargy, sexual indifference, bingeing, insomnia, shouting at the children, crying, backache, headache, digestive troubles. Medication may be prescribed and can be helpful in crisis management. What you chiefly need, however, is someone skilled to talk to. If your doctor does not offer to arrange for psychotherapy *ask* for it. Avoid amateur groups but MIND and the Samaritans can help. Professional counselling by itself is usually enough to lift the mental murk.

There is also action you can take on your own. Reinforce your daily habits, for instance; or seek a period of positive relaxation – meditation, reading, painting. And try to be with other people some of the time.

Religion and philosophy have the best maps and usually supply social support but altruism also offers an outside motivation and distraction. Help others, it will help you too.

47 PARKINSON'S DISEASE
A modern medical miracle

Parkinson's disease is common among older people, and as the world's population ages we shall see more of it. In recent years drugs have been found that control it, though they don't cure it unfortunately – thus the prescription is for life.

The disease arises when certain brain cells, which secrete a chemical called dopamine, die off – atrophy. The treatment is to dose the patient with artificial dopamine, plus other chemicals that carry it to the brain.

The cause, in most cases, is unknown. However, researchers are tentatively suggesting that it may be due to the gradual accumulation of some poison over many years. This would explain why it occurs so frequently among people over the age of 55. It is *not* now considered to be part of the normal ageing process.

What then could the poison be? Many theories have been advanced, but no proof is yet forthcoming.

Could it be an excess of metals in the diet? The similarity of certain metal poisonings makes this a strong possibility. Manganese, copper and some other chemicals cause Parkin-

---

A HISTORIC DISCOVERY

★ James Parkinson was a remarkable man. Apart from his historic description of the disease, he published works on fossils, dangerous sports, the improvement of trusses and the regulation of madhouses. He narrowly escaped deportation to Australia for reformist activities.

★ Parkinsonism can result from Wilson's disease (the inability to excrete copper), manganese poisoning, strokes, tumours and encephalitis lethargica.

★ Parkinson's disease is one of the very few conditions that seems to be partly alleviated by cigarette smoking. Doctors suggest this is because tremors decrease with intentional movement.

★ Parkinsonian tremor disappears during sleep, although patients may often have trouble with insomnia.

★ One theory for the cause of schizophrenia is the 'dopamine hypothesis': in other words, too much dopamine in the brain causes schizophrenia; too little causes Parkinson's.

Common symptoms

If you or someone you know starts to show signs of Parkinson's, see the GP for diagnosis and treatment. Here are a few symptoms:

★ Tremor, usually first involving finger and hand. 'Pill-rolling' with thumb and forefinger is common.

★ Rigidity and jerkiness of movement.

★ Slowness and lack of precision of movement.

★ Monotonous speech.

★ Shuffling gait.

These symptoms don't necessarily mean you have the disease. Remember you can't diagnose yourself – leave it to the experts.

---

sonian symptoms – a recent case from America has been reported of a young man developing the disease after ingesting a home-made hallucinatory drug.

Manganese being one suspect, it is worth noting that foods rich in manganese include coffee, cocoa, some breakfast cereals, whole wheat, oats, nuts, rice and, particularly, *tea*! Many vitamin and mineral preparations contain the metal, so check the labels. Fear not that you may become short of manganese – manganese deficiency is virtually impossible to achieve.

Aluminium has also been named, as it has for Alzheimer's disease. Rich sources include spinach, some cheese, salmon, milk, some breakfast cereals again, coffee, cocoa and once again, particularly, *tea*! We use aluminium pans much of the time, so these might be another source. Unlikely, but aluminium serves no dietary purpose!

Tension and stress may play a part in the cause. The section of your brain containing the dopamine cells is called the basal ganglia, situated at the lower back of your head. Perhaps neck tension constricts the flow of fluids. Regular, gentle exercise and massage of the neck is always valuable, in any case.

Parkinson's has a slight genetic component, so if there is a history of it in your family, you'll have more cause to think about these theories, which is all they are at present, and help the cause of research into the disease so that firm knowledge can replace theory.

Drugs have certainly made an enormous difference to patients' lives. The handling of Parkinson's has been one of the wonders of modern pharmacology.

DIABETES
Good control = long life

Gary Mabbutt plays football for Tottenham and England. He is also a diabetic. It *is* possible, with good control, for diabetics to live full and active lives. What's more, by diagnosing the disease early, you can effectively prevent the tragic consequences of diabetes in later life, such as heart disease, kidney failure and blindness.

Diabetes occurs when the pancreas fails to secrete enough insulin. Insulin maintains the level of sugar in the blood; inadequate insulin results in excess blood sugar.

There are two types of common diabetes: Type I (Insulin Dependent Diabetes) and Type II (Non Insulin Dependent Diabetes) – IDD and NIDD. IDD usually affects younger people; NIDD the middle-aged and beyond. The two types have different features and different treatments. But both benefit from dietary restriction and general good health . . . so if you've

---

DIABETES FACTS

★ Diabetes gets its name from the Greek. It means 'flowing through'. This refers to the common symptom of polyuria.

★ Undiagnosed male diabetics sometimes notice white flecks on their shoes. These are traces of dried sugar from the urine. One such person actually took his shoes back to the shop, complaining that they were faulty.

★ It has been noticed that the urine of diabetics is attractive to flies. This again is because of the sugar therein.

★ Many people are horrified by animal experimentation, but the successful modern treatment of diabetes has involved the sacrifice of many animals. Until the discovery of insulin in the 1920s, diabetes was often a fatal disease.

★ There is a family link between diabetes, thyroid disease and pernicious anaemia. Although it is rare for a person to have all three, anyone with a blood relative who has one of them, is at greater risk of developing one of the three.

got either, stop smoking, stop overeating and start exercising. Tell your doctor what you are doing so that, if necessary, she can adjust your treatment.

The symptoms of diabetes include polyuria (peeing too much), polydypsia (drinking too much), tiredness, lack of sexual interest and menstrual problems. If in doubt, see your GP. In IDD, weight loss is common, but not in NIDD, which commonly affects the obese.

Most authorities now consider that diabetes is an immune disease, probably caused by the immune system attacking the body. This is called auto-immunity. Diabetes also has a genetic component. If any of your blood relatives are diabetic, you have more reason to consider the possibilities. (It has been estimated that half of Britain's diabetics are not diagnosed.)

Because of the immune involvement, there may be a link with allergy. Try eliminating certain foods from your diet, always bearing in mind that you *must* feed yourself properly, and that positive results might not appear for some months.

Treatment of IDD (Type I) is, by definition, based on insulin. This was formerly extracted from the frozen pancreases of pigs and cattle. Human, cloned insulin is now available as well. There are different preparations of insulin, so you should not hesitate to experiment (under your doctor's supervision) until you find the right one for you.

You will also have to watch your diet. Many people find this difficult, but it is essential for your long-term health. After all, what's a bar of chocolate set against 20 years of extra life?

NIDD can be treated by other drugs and diet, but many people can manage with diet alone. Remember, you may have to sacrifice cake, but you'll certainly be able to manage the finest French cuisine (in moderate quantities). With a little fore-thought and care, you can eat food as delicious as you could wish for.

Lastly we come to Public Enemy No. 1 (you've guessed it: the little cancer sticks) and Public Friend No. 1 (a walk, a run or a swim). Diabetes predisposes to heart disease and stroke, two of the Three Big Killers. This is even more reason to substitute exercise for tobacco. Indeed, late onset diabetes may even save lives if it shocks people into changing their habits. Don't rush it with the fitness, though. Build up slowly – Gary Mabbutt didn't step straight from an office job into the national team. There is even evidence that unduly vigorous exercise can be dangerous for diabetics – it can lead to 'hypoglycaemia' (*low* blood sugar). However, bad food habits are the prime cause of 'hypos', so eat properly.

Your GP will be well experienced in the long term management of diabetes. Consult him regularly, and get your urine checked once a year.

49
CANCER IN MIDDLE AGE
Deaths that can be avoided

Certain cancers predominate in the 30 to 50 age groups: for men, it is cancers of the stomach, lung, colon and rectum; for women, of the ovary, breast, cervix and uterus. Skin cancer affects both sexes in this group.

Many lives could be saved of these people, who are just past their prime and have much to give yet.

Cancer scientists say 35 to 80 per cent of all cancer deaths could be stopped *now* by simply changing our ways.

It's true that some cancers have direct causes – a virus (eg: Burkitt's lymphoma), a chemical (asbestos) or a gene gone 'wild' – but most develop after years of subtle bodily abuse that weakens the immune systems. This abuse is in the things we can control: what we eat, how much we drink, and whether we smoke.

Help your immune system, which bears the brunt of fighting cancer, in helping to ward off this disease of the middle-aged. With lung cancer your risk rises and falls with the number of cigarettes smoked and how deeply you inhale – it is never too late to stop.

Women are now entering the lung cancer bracket, through the increasing spread of the cigarette habit across the sexes. Other common cancers in women can be checked with regular examinations:

★ Breast cancer. It calls for monthly self-examination and regular screening. (Turn to Way 74 for details on how to carry out self-examination. It's very straightforward.)

★ Cervical and uterine cancers. Have a smear test done regularly.

★ Ovarian cancer. Women should have an annual bi-manual pelvic examination, done with two hands, to examine the abdomen both inside and out *at the same time*. It's the way to pinpoint abnormality.

For men's stomach and colon cancer: apart from changing eating habits, drink in moderation only, for heavy drinking greatly increases risk. Of course, drinking too much has other side effects. If you are worried about whether you are drinking to much, see Way 52.

No one can be guaranteed freedom from cancer, but follow those guidelines to reduce the risks.

Remember, early treatment of cancer offers a better chance of cure.

50

SCHIZOPHRENIA
A cry from the heart

There is little firm or final about schizophrenia, among other mental diseases, except that it is a horrific condition both for patients and their families. The cause is unknown, the diagnosis often doubtful and the treatment a source of disagreement between different authorities and experts.

In general, though, it can claim to be a major component of the official list of deaths due to mental disorders each year – more than 10,000. But you can safely guess a far larger figure, realizing that schizoid patients are at a high risk from violence and exposure when they are in the grip of the disease and also that their general physical health and nutrition are badly affected. They are more likely to die from the effects of smoking even. Surveys show that their cigarette intake is well above the national average.

So grave danger is always lying in wait for these patients.

The disputes about the disease start at the beginning. Has the person in fact developed it or not? Some of the most notable psychiatric medics of the age, such as the late Donald Winnicot, believed the patient should never be 'labelled' as a schizophrenic.

In the very opposite camp is the Schizophrenia Association of Great Britain, which says that people with schizophrenia in the family ought to 'stand up and be counted'.

The association also accuses psychiatrists of having quite given up with schizophrenics. One can understand the impatience of the association, whose members are mostly drawn from sufferers or their families, for progress to be made in nailing down the disease, but it's easy also to appreciate the viewpoint of the medical researchers who will not act until they have solid conclusions to work on.

Sensibly, the association is putting its own weight into supporting research as well as polemics, and has backed a fellowship at a Welsh university whose brief is to work on the question of whether schizophrenia is biologically determined. They think that the cause might be in body chemicals that go wrong and that these chemicals are inherited.

Certainly if this can be proved it will be a large step towards discovering the cure as well as the cause. This is why the association emblazons on its banner the words 'Schizophrenia is conquerable!'

Sadly, until research is speeded up and can deliver an answer there are only palliatives at hand, not cures – other than time itself, which often will work a miracle.

WAYS

51~60

HABITS AND ADDICTIONS

A bad habit is like an old friend you can't stand. You want to give it up, you know it's not doing you any good, but a perverted sense of loyalty keeps you at it. Friends, however awful, have one big advantage – they're not likely to feed you to the sharks. But some bad habits will.

Everyone knows that cigarettes are horrid, that alcohol can make you miserable, that gambling can cost you your sanity . . . even your house. Not everyone can offload the burden easily, despite the fact that it might bring the Moment of Truth 20, 30 or even 50 years nearer. The best way to change is, most likely, to get involved with other people. Alcoholics should get to AA, gamblers to GA, and sniffers should join Families Anonymous. You're not alone in this desire to reform – just muse on the number of cigarettes stubbed out with irrevocable finality at about 2 am on New Year's morning!

Try making a pact with a friend or relative: the first to start smoking again pays the other £500. It may seem like a lot, but it's peanuts really. Money won't buy you a new pair of lungs or a fresh liver. Religion, politics, beauty, fame . . . even genius is no escape. A bronchial carcinoma has no respect for its host's accomplishments or qualities. It loves only tobacco, and will kill to feed this insatiable appetite.

Youth and its foolishness are often to blame. So many kids start smoking and drinking, not to mention sniffing, before they know any better. The next thing you know they aren't kids any more, just sick, sad adults. Sometimes corpses. Show your kids that there's another way: give up smoking for their sake, keep the top on the bottle, talk to them about the problems of growing-up.

If you're the obsessive type, turn your mind elsewhere. Life is full of exotic and delicious pleasures that don't cost much, and won't cost you your life.

Not today, not tomorrow, not next week nor next year. If you've got a deadly habit, bite the bullet. A few weeks of discomfort has to be better than the terminal ward.

ADDICTION TO WORK
. . . and how to enjoy it

Work is undergoing a revolution. The new technologies make the prospect of the workerless factory quite feasible. Yet we need work. The oldest survivors have mostly worked hard. It's been a habit with them, and a good one.

We must always work, however sophisticated technology becomes. Food must be grown and distributed, houses built, babies delivered, bodies buried – even the computers need tending and feeding. It is to be hoped that we will be able to work less, perhaps. Certainly, a major objective must be to make work more enjoyable. We must have music – so the musicians will have to work hard for our pleasure. Actors will work to create the films and plays to enrich our leisure hours.

Most people, particularly those with menial jobs, want to work less. And why not? Longer holidays, the 30-hour week . . . perhaps society can aim at the 3-day week with full pay for everybody by the year 2000. It's up to us all to start thinking now about ways to give us greater freedom and more time.

In the meantime, work must be made more interesting and less stressful. This is an essential health concern; no matter how hard you diet and exercise, there's not much point if your job makes you depressed. Put a little thought into it, a little planning and a lot of discussion with your workmates. Long-term dividends are guaranteed.

LIFE'S WORKS

★ A few notorious workers: Bach, who went blind in later life – from too much composing by candlelight?; Mozart, who wrote more than 600 works, including a number of full-length operas, in his 35-year lifespan; Fermat, who developed major mathematical theories (in the fields of number, probability and analytical geometry) during his time off from work as a lawyer; Borodin, who achieved greatness in both music and chemistry.

★ George Stephenson worked down a Whitehaven coal pit from the age of 7 to the age of 89. After three years' retirement, he died at 92.

★ When China was liberated in 1949 large numbers of peasants had to be taught how to *play*. Their lives had been so oppressed and bestial that they had no notion of such activity.

52
ALCOHOL
A bit of booze – but not too much

'Take a little wine for thy stomach's sake,' wrote St Paul, and who would argue with such a distinguished commentator? Keep the emphasis on the little!

There are many benefits to be obtained from a wee dram, a fact well known to a large percentage of the world's population. In some religions alcohol is respected, just to re-emphasize the point of its value . . . and its danger. Your personal and social lives can respond well; your circulatory, digestive and nervous systems ditto. The great secret is moderation.

What is a moderate ration of alcohol? This depends, to a certain degree on the drinker. Women generally cannot tolerate as much as men. The size of the person is another factor. There again, some can just take a lot more liquor, without obvious damage to the health, for no understood reason. For the general population, it has been reckoned that one and a half fluid ounces a day is OK – that's two pints, or four whiskies. But it varies, so in the end you can only work it out for yourself.

Choosing the right alcohol is important. Some people love a sherry, but can't drink port. Others thrive on white wine and detest rum. Cost is a big factor for the less well off, but even two cognacs a day, if you buy a bottle from the supermarket, will

THE DRINKING CLASSES

★ In a study of murders in Northern Ireland a doctor found that half the murderers were drunk at the time – and so were 40 per cent of the murdered!

★ The highest death rate in the world from alcohol-induced cirrhosis is found in Chile – 50 per 100,000. The lowest is Iceland, with 1 per 100,000.

★ Throughout the world alcoholic spirits are made from a wide variety of substances: including cactus, water melon, raspberries, pears, pineapples and milk.

★ If a person is suffering from methanol (wood alcohol) poisoning, give him a stiff alcoholic drink before taking him to hospital. This lessens the toxic effects of the methanol.

★ Many drug-related deaths involve the abuse of liquor.

★ Alcohol kills ten times as many teenagers as heroin.

Children and liquor

There's been a lot in the Press of late concerning school-age drinking. No doubt many of the young fools will graduate to full alcoholism, ruining their lives and costing the NHS huge sums.

Don't encourage kids to drink. Most people wouldn't give liquor to a dog, so why intoxicate a child? Children really prefer playing games and good dinners. Don't force adulthood on them – they have a lot to teach us. Alcohol can easily ensnare anyone, even more so a youngster, who has little sense of future or responsibility.

only set you back about 60p. Don't economize, if you're putting your health at risk – quality liquor is easier on the system than cheap.

Immoderate use of alcohol is a horror. It can damage you from head (mental illness) to toe (gout). And all the parts between . . . and the damage to your emotional and social relations (as with divorce). Alcohol can become an obsession as deadly as heroin. An American actress recalled how she once cradled a bottle in her arms, cooing fondly: 'You're my only friend.' Only Alcoholics Anonymous saved her from an early grave.

If you are an alcoholic, there is but one cure – total abstinence. AA, doctors, psychiatrists, clinics and other institutions can help, but the ready availability of the poison puts the main burden on the individual. If you really can't give up, consider emigrating to Saudi Arabia.

It helps to try and find the cause for alcoholism. There can often be emotional or other reasons that have never been properly understood. Lack of faith in life and the world may have something to do with it, and many alcoholics find salvation in religion. This is no bad thing – remember that churches have smaller advertising budgets than breweries.

For some people there can be no moderate drinking. *Don't* feel obliged to drink, just because your friends do. It's quite possible to enjoy a night out or a party without liquor, and many have lived long, full and happy lives as teetotallers. If you are the addictive type (you'll probably know), it might be wise to confine yourself to an occasional swig. Getting well plastered once a month may make you feel rotten in the morning, but it won't hurt you as much as regular sozzling. And it won't put you at risk of sliding into oblivion. Be warned, it's quite easy to become an alcoholic, even if you haven't got much money. As Paul said: a *little* wine.

DRUGS
Kicking the habit

We are surrounded by the temptation of drugs. Not just the illegal ones, but cigarettes, alcohol and prescribed drugs. Neither tea nor coffee have any identifiable nutritional value, so they too ought to be classified as drugs.

Drugs can be useful – even heroin, which is prescribed for the severe pain of such serious diseases as cancer. But most can be dangerous, often extremely dangerous. This applies to prescribed drugs as well: some anti-depressants can kill in overdose, and many have questioned the long-term use of tranquillizers such as valium. Indeed, some authorities consider that the overall health of the population is due less to modern drug therapy than to improved nutrition, sewerage, housing and so forth. Whereas much of modern illness can be directly attributed to drug abuse.

Giving up drugs can be difficult – and some much more than others. At the root of all addiction, though, is the same problem: *you*. Only you can take the decision to escape your particular prison. You can get help, you can read books, you can talk about it all day long; in the end you, and you alone, have to choose. Choose, in many cases, between life and death.

DOPE ON DRUGS

★ It has been estimated that as many people are killed by prescribed drugs as by traffic accidents.

★ The founder of modern chemotherapy was Paul Ehrlich. After testing thousands of compounds he came up with salvarsan, a chemical that included arsenic. It was effective against the dread disease, syphilis.

★ The use of benzodiazepines (such as valium) in pregnancy has led to some birth defects in babies.

★ Marijuana affects memory and mood, often quite dramatically. But it does not seem to affect physical coordination. A study in the West Indies showed that, whereas alcohol definitely increased your chances of having a traffic accident, marijuana did not.

★ Sigmund Freud took cocaine in his youth. A friend of his was killed by the drug, and Freud subsequently forswore it for life.

Replace your dependence with other things. Exercise, hobbies, a new job, love, religion, politics, emigration, meditation, psychotherapy, study, dance or music. Join a support group. Seek out the best medical advice. Whatever you try, you'll be left alone one day, just you and the tablet, or the needle. It's a personal battle, and only you can win it.

Miles Davis replaced heroin with music. He dedicated himself to his band and trumpet. Only *after* he knocked the poison on the head did his true genius emerge. He did it the hard way – cold turkey. He bit the bullet.

Here is a short list of addictive drugs; not all, strictly speaking, are addictive but they are all harmful to mind and body. Avoid them.

Heroin Psychoanalysis, apparently, has helped a number of distinguished jazz musicians to give it up. Cold turkey, sweating it out, is tough, but many have succeeded. There are new treatments available, such as electrical stimulation.

Cigarettes By far the biggest killer – one estimate puts the annual toll at 80,000 lives. (See Way 54.)

Cocaine Dangerous, not just because of sudden death from heart failure, but also because of serious psychological and emotional problems. If you're rich you're at greater risk, owing to cocaine's high cost. If you're a serious addict, try giving your money to charity – you'll be better off.

Amphetamine Getting more common, and cheaper than cocaine. But just as deadly.

Valium and related tranquillizers Very difficult to kick. Some people have continued using them for five years or more after the need has gone. Dangers are subtle, but real.

Alcohol Tricky, owing to low cost and easy availability. (See Way 52.)

Glue and solvents Mostly adolescents. Cheap and available. Can be very dangerous. Parents should try and probe the underlying reasons for the child's problem, and deal sympathetically with it. (See Way 56.)

LSD and other hallucinogens Psychologically dangerous. Not strictly addictive.

Marijuana Psychologically dangerous if used for any length of time. Mildly physically addictive. The problem of 'leading on' to more dangerous drugs.

Anti-depressants Not particularly addictive, but harmful. To be fair, they have saved lives in serious cases of depression.

Doctors are aware of the problem of 'multiple addiction', and you should be too. It's quite common for a person to smoke, drink, use heroin, cocaine, marijuana and prescribed drugs, all on a daily basis. One drug can feed another. If you want to stop smoking, it could help to cut down on coffee and tea.

105

THE TRAVELS OF NOSMO KING
Cigarettes, no!

A stranger from a far-off epoch was one day travelling up the length of Britain on a crowded express train. The train, pride of BR, was speeding along, barely swaying, above a beautiful green valley. The stranger introduced himself to the man on the seat opposite. 'Excuse me,' he said, 'my name is Nosmo. Can you tell me something about this bridge we're traversing, this splendid structure?'

'Yes, I can, it's the longest bridge in the country,' said the Britisher, 'and the highest too.' He leaned forward to shake hands. 'I'm John Smith, by the way,' he added, and announced very proudly, 'from the Inland Revenue,' indicating a glossy black briefcase over his head.

The train continued flying along the bridge while they drank a friendly cup of tea together. Suddenly Nosmo the stranger jumped to his feet, knocking Mr Smith's cup flying, and made to dash up the aisle. But too late! He'd seen a young chap suddenly shove the carriage door open and step out into the void, gone for ever. A railway guard respectfully closed the door again.

Nosmo was in a dreadful state of shock. A number of the other passengers were not a little upset, too, as they peered out of the windows to watch the body tumbling down to the rocks so far below. They shook their heads sorrowfully.

Nosmo shuddered and said to his neighbour: 'Won't the driver stop? Shall I pull the cord?'

'No point. Nothing he can do,' said Mr Smith shortly, 'very difficult country around here.'

'There's another!' shrieked Nosmo, darting up once again – and once again too late. Mr Smith, unperturbed, continued reading pleasurable extracts from his tax magazine.

Then a young woman brushed past them and she too hurled herself through the train door.

FAG-ENDS

★ About 80,000 smoking related deaths occur per year. This is about one in seven of all deaths.

★ Women on average live five years longer than men. The explanation may simply be that there are a greater number of deaths from smoking among the males.

★ Very few doctors smoke but some 47 per cent of nurses still do.

Help from the state

According to Government figures published early in 1987 smoking related illness costs the NHS £370 million a year.

To help counter this about £10 million was spent on official anti-smoking campaigns (and several times that amount by the tobacco industry, which we can interpret as going on pro-smoking campaigns). Look at this financial estimate, then.

Cost of publicity on smoking: Assume £100 million on cigarette advertising, then the *net* pro-smoking advertising charge is £90,000,000.

Cost of looking after victims: £370 million. Estimate cost due to loss of labour by the victims as approximately an equal amount, i.e. £370 million. Total £740 million – eight times the anti-smoking budget.

The solution is clear: step up the anti-smoking campaign – and ban tobacco advertising. Down would go the number of people smoking, down would go the cost of the NHS and down would go taxes.

'What are you all up to, sitting there so calmly?' implored Nosmo of the other passengers.

'Quite right,' one of them replied, tut-tutting, 'a woman too. It's a terrible waste. They've been told about it, mind. They've been warned that throwing themselves out of the train can be damaging to their health, but they are unable to stop themselves. It's a sort of mild drug, you know.'

'So young, some of them,' lamented Nosmo, 'have they no hope for life?'

'So young! Schoolboys and schoolgirls many of them are,' nodded a man next to him, 'they like to show off that they are just as adult as the rest of us . . . and have as little will-power. No, they can't stop themselves.'

'Doesn't the state attempt to stop them, then, forbid them travelling this route, say?' asked Nosmo desperately.

'No, no, my dear Nosmo,' Smith intervened, reprimanding him gently, 'there is an advantage to the state, after all – they pay taxes to go like that. Quite important revenue it represents.'

'Taxes?' echoed the stranger from another time-and-logic warp. 'What are the taxes for?'

'Let me explain to you. The taxes are to maintain the hospitals that care for those who are rescued from the valley below and are but maimed. Some of them, you know, survive quite some time, but they are in dreadful pain as their lives draw to a close and have to be lovingly tended.'

PROMISCUITY
A 3-letter word rears its lovely head

In the field of addiction sex is no exception. The more you have of it, the more you desire . . . and thereafter the series continues: over-indulgence, promiscuity, addiction. As always, addiction is painful and counter-productive, at the least.

However, though not true for drugs, a minimum amount of sex is very advantageous to us all, except perhaps for holy men and those unfortunates not equipped with perfect sets of chromosomes.

Sex is necessary for a full, rounded life, of course, but also for keeping the body's drives and functions in a sound state. (Not to mention its role in the reproduction of the species, though one fears that science might soon enough try to hijack that happy property from us!)

A nice balance is what's needed.

Too much, overdoing it, shopping around, indiscriminate adventurings – in a word promiscuity – will bring about your

---

TOO MUCH OF A GOOD THING

★ Giovanni Giacomo Casanova the infamous womanizer, who used this particular talent as a means of support, actually studied for the church before he was expelled for immorality.

★ Georges Simenon, the creator of Maigret, arranged for a different woman to be sent up to him every night for many years.

★ The Japanese geisha (meaning 'art person') girl is not a prostitute but an entertainer who has studied and is gifted in the art of conversation, music, dance and singing.

★ Relationships other than monogamous are considered promiscuous in the Western world, though many other societies allow them.

★ Unlike other basic drives such as hunger or thirst, gratification of the libido can be postponed or transferred without endangering the individual's existence.

★ Promiscuous behaviour can lead to the birth of many children. In the eighteenth century the Emperor of Morocco fathered more than 1000 children.

The virtues of being virtuous

Moral reinforcement is probably the soundest method to consider in your attempt to prevent yourself falling into the trap of promiscuity. Whatever your bag, Christian, heathen, beggarman, thief, you need to apply the appropriate wise thoughts and disciplinary devices of your creed.

Remember, too, the practical side. You pay a heavy price always, when you go on the loose, even without the new bogey of AIDS.

Therefore keep a glass of water handy, so that when you feel the urge coming on you can follow that old piece of homely advice: take a glass of water instead.

downfall. Where marriage tones down the edge of appetite so that after some months of glorious honeymoon the average couple soon descends to a twice-a-week level, or even joins the Saturday night club, a promiscuous career elevates sex to such a degree of hyperactivity that it begins to invade the centre of life. Application to your work is affected, social values are eroded and there is even a danger of serious disease.

Too little is also not going to suit those imperious genes. It's in obedience to their demands that the body finds such pleasure in sex; forcing it to go out and look for a mate. If we should refuse to respond to the need, Nature begins to lose interest in us. It allows various bodily functions to run down. Medical science therefore now prescribes for a range of conditions a more active interest in sex: to counter osteoporosis, the thinning of bones, to improve a woman's condition after menopause, to be recruited in the fight against stress and insomnia, even in the cause of aerobics – and of course in fostering long-term partnerships.

Sex is one of the ingredients of a healthy life as well as a happy one, so you must not let it fade. For if sex can become addictive, certainly the opposite is true, that if you don't have it at all, you soon find you don't miss it. That explains how the monks and other celibates can manage on their diet of zero sex. No, the opposite of promiscuity is not after all celibacy, which is merely its other extreme, but single-couple caring.

Not too much, not too little! That's the message, as so often. It means we may need to strike a position somewhere between the rigidity of traditional marriage and the state of promiscuity so beloved of the media, and so aired by them, of casual couplings and recouplings one atop another. They make it sound so normal and OK. But it is not, today the pendulum of opinion is settling midway between the poles, promiscuity is no longer the fashionable ideal . . . and it's no longer safe.

109

YOUTHFUL SNIFFING
Solvents ... and solutions

Remarkably, the experts on solvent-sniffing find it not so dangerous and damaging a phenomenon as do the general public and parents. They see it like this: though as many as a quarter of school children have a try at it, very few indeed are trapped by the habit. What's more, even those addicted, invariably the ones with serious behaviour problems at home, suffer little long-term harm.

Consider alcohol, by contrast: as many as nine out of ten children have tried it and *millions* become addicts when they grow up. What's more, those addicted suffer effects both grave and widespread, linked to death in scores of ways: road accidents, murder, suicide, liver disease . . .

Finally, sniffers can mostly be cured, whereas alcoholics may linger on as such for ever. Perhaps the worst that can be said about chronic sniffers is that they could easily turn into alcoholics.

Nevertheless the abuse of solvents or volatiles does lead to

SIGNS OF SNIFFING

★ Solvent sniffing has caused the following unpleasant conditions: suffocation; choking on one's vomit; brain damage; fits and kidney damage.

★ Sniffers tend to be boys rather than girls. Perhaps this is to do with adolescent sexual maturation and the accompanying problems.

★ Signs of sniffing in children include: excitable groups of boys around the bike-sheds or in isolated corners of playgrounds; giggling; truanting; early morning irritability; dry coughs, runny noses and watery eyes; lots of empty crisp bags lying about.

★ One study has shown that 27 per cent of sniffing deaths were caused by glues; 24 per cent by gas fuels (mainly butane); and 17 per cent by aerosol sprays. Of the dead, 72 per cent were under 20; 95 per cent were male.

★ Fashion is one of the strong influences in turning youngsters to sniffing for the first time; hidden emotional disturbance will turn it into a habit.

deaths in the young, the main victims; the number dying in Britain has grown year by year until it is now at about 100 (fewer than from acute alcoholic poisoning in the young). These are some of the sniffable items, ordinary workaday products, responsible for these tragedies:

Lighter fuel	Plaster removers
Glues	Typewriter fluid
Anti perspirants	Glitter lamp fluid
Cleaners and thinners	Chloroform
Fly sprays	Petrol
Paint sprays	Hair sprays

The way to sort it out? According to Dr Joyce Watson, who spent 12 years as the confidante of young sniffers in Glasgow, there has to be a whole range of options. In deciding which to apply one must first come to the understanding that the problem is about adolescents coping with loss and pain. The victims she encountered had been hurt by adoption, a parent's suicide, a parent's death and such heavy blows.

For this reason, for any therapeutic programme to be successful the parents must be involved.

57

JUNK FOODS
Train the appetite to reject 'em

What's good to eat and what's bad is a very confused subject. At the top the medical profession itself is not really settled as to whether fats, sugar and salt, to name but three little villains, are harmful or not. At the other end many a self-appointed guru holds violent opinions against meat of any sort or confectionery in any form, or believes most passionately in the forced feeding of fibre or vitamins or in overdoses of minerals such as zinc. Is either side right? You must take your pick which you believe in, if any. Argue both sides at the same time and you'll still be fashionable.

It seems magic rather than science still reigns – like primitive peoples we have faith that nibbling this or that item of food will work amazing cures or curses, and we blindly follow our pet wizard.

These experts agree on one thing: the denouncing of junk foods. Yet that is the source of the greatest confusion. Before condemning it, how do we define it? Hamburgers, crisps, ice cream, chocolate bars, fizzy drinks? Chips with everything? Are these the culprits? And if so, why?

Have these foods been tested? Are they safe? Or are they only lacking in nutrition, and therefore harmful in that they shut out nutritious foods?

But it does not need a trained researcher to point out that one thing all junk foods have in common is their *convenience*: they

---

THE NEW BISCUIT MIX

Here is the list of ingredients of the miniature Club Biscuits, given away at petrol stations, as advertised on the package:

Milk chocolate flavoured coating 50% (sugar, vegetable fat and butter, dried skimmed milk, cocoa mass, whey powder, emulsifier lecithin, flavouring)

Flour
Sugar (again)
Animal and vegetable fat, including hydrogenated
    vegetable oil
Glucose syrup
Salt
Emulsifier lecithin (again!)
Flavouring (again!)
Colour caramel.

---

must be conveniently pick-uppable anywhere and at any hour, to be eaten on the spot. Most important, they must be conveniently manufacturable in massive quantities, at a massive profit, and distributable world wide.

The pre-manufactured junk food will have preservatives added (adding at the same time an unpleasant tang), and extra flavour or colour stirred in, in an unconvincing attempt to replace the lost natural fresh qualities. In turning out a convenience item, you thus do terrible harm to its taste, disguise it how you may. Yes, the real crime of junk is that it is unappetizing compared to the real, the natural. Ever noted the difference between a limp hamburger and a steak newly grilled? Or squeezed fresh orange for its juice and compared this to the packaged stuff? But it's harder work to grill or squeeze than to pick up. Much more convenient, oh yes.

Be guided by your taste, disciminate with a trained palate and you'll willingly lay off junk foods. It's actually worth buying new-baked bread daily, as the French do, for the glorious taste of it; it's worth podding green peas for the treat in eating them.

However, if you still need to buy sliced bread or eat lunch standing up in a quick-food joint from time to time, there is no great need to worry. It's only your reputation that will suffer, not your health. It's a pity to have to give junk food any good marks, but that is so; there is useful protein even in an assembly-line hamburger, useful energy in a pack of white sugar and useful carbohydrate in any loaf. Fibre? If you are sure to take in plenty of vegetables, salads and fresh fruit and other *in*convenience foods you will get quite enough of that. As for vitamins, you need no bottled supplements anyway, unless you suffer from some rare vitamin disease.

At the most a few less significant trace constituents are lost in the convenience processing. Our inner appetite discerns this, without quite knowing how, and adjusts its intake. A human being, guided by the taste buds in his tongue, which in turn are wired to the needs of the body, soon tires of any one dish and goes looking for variety. He switches to other dishes, in this way meeting his spread of requirements.

There may be risk for anyone very young and obstinate who exists *purely* on crisps of different flavours, say, with an occasional fizzy drink, but is there such a person outside the *Guinness Book of Records*? And there may also be exceptions among those very faddists searching for long-life magic. The ultra vegetarian or fibre-freak, for instance, may unintentionally be starved of certain nutritive essentials. Was there not the classic case of the man who died from an exclusive diet of 'health-giving' carrot extract? Still, it wasn't junk food that killed him.

58

MINDPOWER
Where there's a will . . . there are 99 ways!

It's quite true there are people luckier than ourselves, born with wealth, wisdom, a place in society . . . even good looks. Don't envy them. The most valuable commodity in life, strength of will, does not have to be inherited, you develop it for yourself, then make a habit of it; *that* will make you wealthy and wise and earn you that place in society. A habit to cultivate!

It will even improve your looks, for good looks are only a reflection of inner and outer fitness, to be gained by quite

---

THE STORY OF PETER

In his late thirties a Londoner, Peter McGhie, took up running to break himself of the habit of smoking, which he felt to be a spoiling influence on his wellbeing. He needed something anyway to help him get rid of that general run-down feeling brought on by inactivity and middle-aged spread.

The cure worked; what's more in the process he became a devoted marathoner. He aimed when turning 40 to attempt records as a veteran in the London Marathon. He joined a club, Highgate Harriers, and trained regularly. Then – for what reason? – his running suddenly slowed. He felt this deep down as a sign his health was affected, though doctors found nothing wrong – it was in his imagination, they maintained.

But he *knew*, as an athlete he could sense the loss of form. His body was not right.

In the end he *was* diagnosed: lung cancer, and almost inoperable. The surgeon said the treatment, with only small chances anyway, would need great will-power to undergo. It was only because he'd given up cigarettes for some time that he had even that chance.

'I'm your man,' volunteered Peter.

He endured the savage chemotherapy cure with forti-tude; within months he was back running slowly, well again. As a mark of gratitude, now aged 40, he eventually entered the marathon; he had himself sponsored for a cancer charity and raced the 26 miles of the race dressed as Will Shakespeare, an allusion to the 'Will' power that had got him back to life.

moderate efforts of will-power.

Finally, the big payoff: in seeking a long and happy life the Way of Will-power is by far the most important of the 99, for it's the one that will help you apply the other 98 Ways of this book.

Will-power is built in many manners, through strength of desire, through fear or hardship, as a forced response to authority, from loyalty, confidence and even distress. It is best applied consciously to achieve a proper purpose in life. Look around at the world to appreciate the marvels, the beauty and the goodness, and aim to win those for yourselves.

How can you build up your strength of will? Long-term by the application of principle, and piecemeal for immediate objectives such as a Sunday jogging session.

Long-term, base your efforts on a conscious philosophical or religious attitude . . . then you are building on a solid foundation. Whole races of humanity have been influenced this way – the Romans, for instance, taught from the mother's knee iron will-power and self-control. If your own mother omitted to impart discipline to you by thrusting your hand in a fire, it can only have been because there was no such item at hand in modern times! In any case today it's self-discipline that we believe in.

Undertake the training work yourself: set the alarm clock for 6 a.m. two days a week, and make use of the extra time in cooking, jogging or studying. It will not only earn you extra wisdom but in the end it will forge you a will of iron.

Study the life of Bonaparte, read the works of Coué, emulate the resolution of the fireworshippers, appreciate the self-discipline of the celibates.

Set yourself definite exercises of the will, for remember the will can be strengthened through training just as well as can the muscles or the memory. Concentrate a few minutes longer on your work, and each day lengthen the period of concentration. Hold off temptation an hour or two longer – or miss it out completely for one cycle.

Go in for a course of study – and stick to it. Invent little tricks to fool yourself out of weaknessess of the will. Put pressure on yourself by announcing to all that you are about to go for a target, make a rod for your back; overload yourself on another target, making a tougher exercise of it.

Learn to persevere in all things you attempt. Perseverance is the royal route to will-power, to developing the inner strength and the confidence that can overcome all opposition. Look at the record of your most-admired politician or your favourite football team: do they not show the power to come back and attack when their backs are against the wall, the ability to go one behind and yet end up on the winning side?

In a crisis it is the one with will-power who survives.

PROCRASTINATION
A thieving old habit

The drug *mañana* – putting off till tomorrow what should be done today – is yet another agent of addiction, a wicked one.

At the very least it robs you of years of life – procrastination, the thief of time. But it's not only time that's lost, it's tempo, the chance to strike while the iron's hot. Putting things off until a more propitious moment, you put off hopes of success, too, of becoming rich, famous or saintly, whichever appeals to you.

Procrastination is only a form of laziness, we must admit that to ourselves first, a form of laziness that can become a sickness. There's even a semi-medical term for it, Oblomovitis. This is from Oblomov, the hero of the novel by Goncharov, who became so addicted to procrastination that finally he couldn't get out of bed in the morning. It starts off as an enchanting comedy but ends as searing tragedy.

Let's have no tragedies like this, dear reader! Make up your mind right now to regain any possible lost ambition and to buckle down with a large notice, DO IT NOW, pinned on the wall.

Become an activist. Clear your In Tray immediately. It's amazing what progress you can make this way. How do you think Caesar became Number One of the Roman scene? Not by putting off his invasion of Ancient Britain until *mañana* . . . he did it today. How do you think Goncharov got into print . . . by first sharpening up all his pencils?

Set yourself standards and rules and stick to 'em. Allow no more than five minutes for a momentary laziness, allow no more than a day for putting off a major step. Load yourself with obligations, broadcast the fact that you are going to do a deed by such and such a time, so you can't get out of it without losing face.

Finally, build forceful deadlines into your life. No one is luckier than a newspaperman, for he has them, he must get his story out by edition time. A marvellous cure for Oblomovitis. It's not surprising to learn that Goncharov himself started his career with articles for the Press.

Fit up deadlines by organizing little payoffs for yourself as well as big ones – a small tipple but not till you finish your task, and another big notice on the wall: 'A sea-going yacht within three years!'

A poet's view of procrastination as being the pinnacle of evil:

'If ever a man indulges himself in murder, very soon he comes to think little of robbing; and from robbing he comes next to drinking and sabbath-breaking, and from that to incivility and procrastination.'

Thomas de Quincy

GAMBLING
A wide range of losing chances

There are 10,000 betting shops in Britain. You can walk into any one, write a few digits on a slip of paper and lose your wage packet in a minute. And many people do!

Then there are casinos, fruit machines, bingo halls, arcades, lotteries, not to mention the Pools, and so forth. The opportunities to lose your money are endless, and the subtleties of the dog, the horse, the card and the wheel can enchant the wisest.

Gambling is an addiction, let's face it. It's not really done for the money. As the famed gambler Dostoevsky wrote: 'The main thing is the play itself . . . greed for money has nothing to do with it.' Indeed, it has often been noticed that gamblers *want* to lose – whatever they might claim. And losing, in the long term, is what they will do. That's how bookies and casinos make their money: the odds are always in their favour.

Giving up is just like giving up any other addiction. You need will-power, patience and, probably, some sort of substitute. For the compulsive gambler, as for the alcoholic, no half-measures will do. Gambler, smoker and drinker are daily tempted. The betting shop nestles snugly between the tobacconist and pub. This opportunity for multiple addiction is grasped by many. Casinos have licences – the mug further dulls his brain on drink and further empties his pocket.

There's also the special case of juvenile gamblers. The need to find cash for their habit leads them to lie, cheat and steal. If not helped, by the time they are 18 they are likely to find themselves in trouble, ending perhaps with custodial sentences.

Lay off your betting

★ For the serious gambler, I recommend professional help: psychotherapy or group counselling.

★ Gamblers Anonymous groups are found in many towns. Contact them if in trouble. Also the Institute for Compulsive Gambling: Tel. 0548–842811, and ask for Rev. Gordon Moody.

★ Rev. Moody has also started a group to cater for Parents of Young Gamblers. Research has shown that children are beginning to play the arcade machines at the age of 13.

★ The Amusement Arcade Action Group, also, campaigns for the passing of laws to control amusement centres.

WAYS
61~70
YOUR MEDICAL SERVICES

As the population ages and our concepts of health broaden the range of medical services increases. Hardly a day passes without some new therapeutic advance, whether it be a fancy feat of surgery or a different way of talking about our problems. In the following pages you'll find a short (and pithy) selection of what's on offer in the longevity marketplace.

Your GP is the first line of defence against the depredations of age – finding a sympathetic doctor, speaking frankly to him (or her) and taking advice in a practical sense will surely keep death and disease from your door.

If you do get ill, you may well face the rigours of NHS hospitals. Are they adequate? I say Yes, resoundingly. Can they be improved? Yes again. Details of private medical schemes are included as well, giving you the chance of finding out what value there is in investing hard-earned cash in life-extension.

Becoming an expert on medical matters is another possibility, even the opportunities of finding employment in health, if you're so inclined. Learn about your immune system, that fantastically subtle and sophisticated weapon that can sometimes turn upon you.

Then there are the alternative types of treatment. Two of the most popular, homeopathy and acupuncture, are dealt with. Only you can decided if they're suitable for you – the one thing to be said is that they are not dangerous.

The mind, as everybody knows, is intimately linked with the body. Psychotherapy, in all its guises, can probably help deal with troubled emotions, and maybe inspire you to a fuller enjoyment of life's riches.

Surgical transplantation is the hard edge of modern medicine. It could be that a new heart, kidney or liver is awaiting you, courtesy of someone else's misfortune.

Lastly, First Aid. Bone up on Airways, Breathing and Circulation and you might just save someone's life – they might do the same for you.

118

61

DIY HEALTH
Self-education in matters medical

Once you take the mystery out of medicine, you'll find there is much useful home doctoring you can do. You can't hope to know everything doctors know, or acquire their wide clinical experience, and you still need to keep regular contact with your GP. But you can make use of a little amateur learning in looking after yourself, and in spite of what they say, a little learning isn't such a bad thing.

Preventive medicine is the best medicine and this is where home knowledge helps. If you want to learn about how to prevent disease and promote 'wellness', start your DIY education with a foray into the extremely complex world of medicine and surgery.

Read an O-level biology textbook; buy a medical dictionary, study a medical textbook, such as the *Oxford Textbook of Medicine*, Davidson's *Principles and Practice*, or Bailey and Love's *Textbook of Surgery*.

Keep up to date, with *The Lancet*, the *BMJ* and other journals – available at libraries. Dig deeper – explore anatomy and physiology. But be warned: don't get obsessive. Hypochrondia can be a serious disease.

And if you're still interested, you could consider a career in the health services.

It takes 10 years to become a surgeon.

Nine years to become a GP.

Midwifery – 4½ years.

Nursing and physiotherapy – 3 years.

Ambulance driver – 2 years.

Never too late to learn

Because of the lengthy training people are reluctant to study medicine after the first flush of youth. But it can be done.

Rosemary Winter qualified as a doctor in her late forties and now practises contentedly in Oxford. All this despite three children, one with Down's syndrome.

Eileen Epstein is another case: at 38, with her kids out of the cradle, she started the long course in dentistry. To this day she dutifully works away at the torture of her patients!

Sue Morris is our third late starter. At the time of writing she was about to qualify as a nurse, aged 44.

If you feel the call, have a go – Dr It Yourself!

62

YOUR GP
Keeping in touch with the family doctor

When in doubt, go and see your GP. Family doctors may seem busy, stern or intimidating, but it's their job to look after your health. Sooner is always better than later, for early diagnosis can improve the course of an illness.

Medical training is probably more rigorous than any other form of education, and generally speaking doctors know most about health. They may not boast of their knowledge, write populist books or sensational articles for the yellow press, but their training ensures that they are experts. It takes at least nine years of grinding work to become a full GP.

However, GPs are just human, so don't expect miracles. What's more, if you don't follow the doctor's orders, you can't expect his cures to be effective. Carry out his instructions about treatment carefully. Take the tablets, refrain from vices and get plenty of rest, if that's what's prescribed.

Look out a doctor who suits you, who you find good. You don't have to be best friends – it's not a doctor's job to massage your ego, but to keep you healthy in mind and body.

A GP's major role is diagnosis. This is a notoriously difficult art – ask any motor mechanic. One study in Leicester found that 'potentially treatable diseases' were missed in 13 per cent of patients. The GP has a whole array of modern diagnostic techniques available – X-rays, immunological tests, computer diagnosis, scanners etc – but clinical diagnosis is still of paramount importance. For this, history-taking is the key. You

DOCTORS' UNUSUAL PRACTICES

★ A Finnish research project has shown that doctors do not live longer than people in comparable social groups. They are obviously not using their knowledge for their own benefit.

★ It has been said that up to 70 per cent of a GP's time is taken up in dealing with emotional and psychiatric problems. In one study, 20 per cent of GPs felt that the majority of their work was 'trivial'.

★ About 22 per cent of GPs are women. This figure will increase considerably in the next few years, with more women entering medical school.

Consulting the doctor

★ Always be totally honest and open with your GP. Doctors have seen more naked bodies than you've had hot dinners. Your embarrassment or shyness about something (such as your bottom) is quite unnecessary, and may even, in the long run, turn out to be dangerous.

★ If you anticipate a physical examination, wear clothes that are easy to remove.

★ Establish a good relationship with your doctor *before* you fall ill – you will be more rational and sensible when well.

★ If in doubt, don't be afraid to ask to see a specialist. Specialists, by definition, know more than GPs about specific areas of medicine. The GP, on the other hand, will know more about you and your situation.

★ For real emergencies, get straight to hospital. Unnecessary night calls on a doctor merely tire him and worsen his daytime work.

★ You don't have to accept treatment from a doctor. But if you refuse treatment, and then drop dead, don't blame her.

★ Be kind to your doctor. One research study has shown that doctors commit suicide twice as often as people in comparable groups.

can help your doctor with frank and full descriptions of your symptoms. Even if they are embarrassing ones, such as blood on the toilet paper or sexual problems, do not hesitate to mention them, as they may indicate underlying disease. It's a good idea to write down your symptoms and questions and refer to these notes during the consultation. And it's *essential* to write down what you are told to do. People quite often forget what they meant to say in the heat of the moment.

Don't be put off by your doctor's manner: it is a difficult job, and they are very busy people. Nevertheless they *are* interested in curing you.

You can change your GP whenever you want and for any reason at all, without asking permission, though you may find it difficult to get on another doctor's list.

One more reason to go and see your GP when you're at all concerned about your health is that it won't cost you a penny. We are fortunate in Britain to have one of the world's best health services, free to all.

THE NHS
It's nationally yours

The hospital service is yours – be satisfied with it and get the best out of it. There is no value in just sitting back criticizing the NHS and praising private medicine; what most people don't realize is that private insurance simply picks out the plums. It won't cover you for many a chronic illness, or psychiatric care or drug and alcohol abuse. Besides, the charges for private doctoring are far above the average person's ceiling.

No chance of the government privatizing this nationally owned asset; and without the NHS there would be little medical care and no major operations at all for the millions. Then you'd be able to talk about queues!

But this does not mean that you the individual should settle for less than the best from the NHS – from its doctors, its nurses and its hospital administrations. Until they ever are privatized, they are *yours*, and there to serve *you*.

With a certain amount of application you can even shop

HOSPITAL NUMBERS

★ An American mental hospital in New York State once housed more than 14,000 beds – enough to drive anyone mad! This has now been reduced to the more humanitarian figure of 3500.

★ St James's in Leeds is the UK's largest general hospital, with 1424 staffed beds.

★ Great Ormond Street Hospital in London was Britain's first children's hospital. Eliza Armstrong, aged 3½, was the first patient to be admitted, on 14 February 1852.

★ The number of hospitals in England declined by 457 (about 20 per cent) between the years 1959 and 1980. The ratio of hospitals per 100,000 people declined in the same period from 5.7 to 4.3 (a drop of 25 per cent).

★ Nurses in Victoria, Australia went on strike for seven weeks in 1986, leaving only skeleton staff in all areas. No patients died from lack of emergency care.

★ Elizabeth Garrett Anderson was the first British woman to obtain a legal qualification in medicine and surgery, in 1865. At the age of 71, she became Britain's first woman mayor.

Improving hospitals

Decent, well-equipped and well-staff hospitals are a necessity. Because they cost so much to build and run, governments constantly try to trim their budgets. In any case many of the rich and powerful use private medicine so resent paying high taxes towards our health care.

But money, though important, is not the only issue. A radical rethinking of hospital procedure is due: more sophisticated nutrition; involvement of staff (and patient!) representatives in broad decision making; more training opportunities for all medical staff; better lighting; fuel efficiency; and more aesthetically pleasing surroundings.

N.B. Many casualty wards have long waiting times – don't bother casualty unless you have a real emergency on your hands.

around for the right hospital, one with a short waiting-list for surgery. *Self-Health Magazine* issues a guide to waiting lists. A Shropshire reader took up their advice and asked his doctor to contact a consultant at a hospital in another district . . . within three weeks he was in and had the operation. This was in spite of having first seen a surgeon privately. This surgeon was very to the point and said if he wanted privileges he would have to pay for them. It was a routine operation, said the surgeon, which could be done in a week for private fees, or would mean 12 months on the NHS waiting list. Well it didn't, through this patient's own private enterprise!

Be enterprising and take an interest. That's a slogan to take you far in the matter of health, as in life generally. It implies two things: look after Number One, but look also after your fellows. Don't be supine, you have rights and you should demand them, for yourself and for others; each of us is as important as the rest. Yes, and the patient is the equal of the doctor or nurse, and entitled to the best treatment.

The check-up is another luxury product of private medicine. But an annual check-up, however thorough, does not come with a guarantee – it is no safeguard against your keeling over the very next day. To conduct comprehensive examinations on everybody is not the answer, but there *are* certain check-ups which are worth pressing for: blood pressure (see Way 76), cervical smears and screening for breast cancer, for instance.

You can certainly ask your GP for a routine check-up, but you cannot insist. But perhaps your wanting a check-up means that you're actually feeling ill though you don't know quite where or what. You could certainly then expect an examination.

64

HOMEOPATHY
Can you find help from 'like with like'?

Homeopathy is one of the more respectable departments of fringe medicine, although still controversial, and it has many successes to boast – in the form of patients still alive today who have relied solely on homeopathic ministerings.

Another success: it has a minority following among conventionally trained doctors. You may consult them at four or five hospitals dotted over Britain or at private clinics.

However, as with the rest of the medical fringe, homeopathy has lost considerable credibility on account of its low published output of scientific study. It makes claims but it rarely seeks to show proof. If its practitioners offered more evidence that their treatments worked, they might be able to convince the sceptics. Instead the question is asked: 'Why do they not? *Is it because they cannot?'*

It is perhaps to protect their vulnerability on this point that homeopaths tend to become involved in ailments where proof is in fact difficult to demonstrate, but depends on the opinion of the patient, conditions such as bad backs where faith often counts for more than measurement, and where in fact faith *can* sometimes work wonders.

Homeopathy is defined in their own words as the practice of

HOPEFUL CURES

★ One homeopathy textbook lists the following conditions as probably incurable by the art: severe psychosis, some types of cancer, severe lacerations and broken leg.

★ A New Zealand practitioner, it is reported, successfully controlled a polio epidemic with gelsemium.

★ A number of homeopathic remedies contain lactose (milk sugar). Those people with lactose intolerance, and there are many, should beware.

★ Calendula lotion is reported to be an effective healing agent for cuts and wounds.

★ Both homeopathy and conventional medicine have used compounds containing arsenic: arsenic trioxide is used in some homeopathic preparations; salvarsan was commonly used to cure syphilis, before the advent of penicillin.

Where to find the practitioners

For those who do want to try homeopathic medicine, contact the Homeopathic Development Foundation's information service on 01–629 3205. They will provide a register of practitioners.

The Royal London Homeopathic Hospital is at Gt Ormond St, WC1: Tel. 01–837 8833.

There are different types of homeopathy practised – find a practitioner you feel comfortable with.

You can buy a short book from your local health food shop. For the student the standard work is *Homeopathic Materia Medica*, edited by W. Boericke.

'treating like with like', a guiding principle too all-embracing for my taste. Their other noteworthy belief is to prescribe remedies 'in infinite dilution'. One benefit claimed for this is that it produces no side-effects. It is not hard to believe; can infinite dilution produce any effects at all?

Homeopathic handbooks contribute to the rather dotty image of the profession. Here's an extract from a guide to the commonest homeopathic medicines and the ailments they're used for:

ACTAEA RAC Despondency. Shooting pains, neuralgia. Stiff neck. Change of life.

CARBO VEG Indigestion with excessive flatulence. Collapse. Hoarseness. Acne. Debility.

KALI BICH Catarrh. Stringy sputum. Pain at root of the nose. Measles.

THUJA Warty growths. Morning headaches. Absence of appetite in the morning.

The most famous remedy of the homeopathists, arnica, is not, oddly enough, covered by their normal principles. It's just a 'speciality'. But it is one that the ordinary population has faith in, too, for the treatment of bruises.

Overall, homeopathy still dwells in an environment faintly coloured with homely superstition. Perhaps its fate is to remain there, for in becoming more rational it would lose its appeal to those desperate to find cures for conditions that medical science has not yet conquered. Old-fashioned magical nostrums may seem the only hope.

There is an insatiable need for some miracle or magic touch among people who cannot find orthodox cures, and they naturally gravitate to the fringe world. Whether wonders are worked or not, they do at least have their attention held while under treatment. That will be a considerable consolation to some.

PSYCHOTHERAPY
Counselling at your local psychomarket

Since the Frenchman Pinel unchained mental patients in the eighteenth century, treatments of psychiatric illness have proliferated. Insulin shock treatment and lobotomy (the surgical separation of the frontal lobes of the brain) have come and gone. Freud and his disciples have changed our perceptions of madness and sanity. Modern drugs have revolutionized the lives of previously incurable schizophrenics. New and better (and worse!) treatment will, no doubt, emerge in the future, for the mind is an infinitely subtle entity.

Mental distress is very common and the cause of much illness and premature death. Apart from obvious dangers, such as suicide and homicide, distress will often affect the will to live. And that will can be worth a good thirty years of extra life.

Psychotherapy, counselling, advice – call it what you will, it is growing daily, and must represent a real need in people. As we all know, a good chat with a friend can help in many problems; a weepy film or a symphony can also do the trick. But in many instances these are not enough, and people turn to agencies of help. This is nothing to be ashamed of: we're all human and vulnerable. It's always better to play it safe. If you think you need help, don't be shy. You can probably bank on the fact that the person you turn to knows all about misery and gloom.

For many people the problem is one of choice. The range of professional services is enormous, from the Catholic confessor, through the social worker and psychiatrist, right to the Reichian therapist. Are they charlatans you may ask yourself? There is no simple answer. Your upbringing and personal preference will condition your choice. A lapsed Catholic may find solace in psychoanalysis; a disillusioned Jew may find the Mass a greater comfort than the Talmud. Anyone may end up in a psychiatric ward, or in a therapy group set up by the local GP. I can only recommend that you keep your mind open, and shop around as best you can in the 'psychomarket'.

Apart from religions, there are many different types of therapy, which fall into three major categories:

1 The talking therapies These include some of the most famous styles, such as Freudian psychoanalysis, with its emphasis on the childhood experiences of the patient. Costs can be as high as £25 an hour or more – and recommended perhaps daily. These therapies are undoubtedly of value, and, no doubt, will continue to flourish in the future. Their appeal may be limited by their cost. Psychoanalysis can take many years and set you back thousands of pounds. It is highly labour-intensive, and will not be generally available until society has undergone a radical change. It is popular with doctors, but then they can afford it!

Your local social worker comes free, but you will not get as much time, nor a therapist with the deep training of a full psychoanalyst. Cheaper, once-a-week psychotherapists, costing maybe £10 an hour, are available in most towns. Ask your GP or social services for details.

2 The touching therapies These derive from the work of Wilhelm Reich, a one-time follower of Freud. The therapies, such as Reichian therapy and Rolfing, are based on the principle that mind and body are one: both must be treated together.

Massage is usual, coupled with talking. Sex therapy is another option: people with sexual problems seek to achieve greater fulfilment under the tutelage of a therapist.

Body therapies are considered part of the holistic health movement, in which the person is treated as a whole. Attention is also paid to diet, exercise and relaxation.

Body therapies make a certain sense, but many of them seem a trifle odd. On the other hand there's nothing wrong with touching. Perhaps our fear of touch is linked to a superstitious fear of contagious disease. Babies and children touch each other very freely. Indeed, without touch, it has been said, babies won't develop contentedly. There's nothing like a good cuddle when you've got the lonesome blues – ask any two-year-old.

There are charlatans galore in this area of psychotherapy . . . the same could be said of many healing practices.

3 The group therapies This category includes the most bizarre organizations, such as Scientology, Primal Therapy and the Orange People. On the other hand, group therapy at a more modest level is often extremely helpful. Gamblers and Alcoholics Anonymous are good practical examples of down-to-earth, useful group therapies. There is also a fashion these days for men and women to form 'Men's' and 'Women's' groups. Reports of these vary, but many seem to be helpful to the members.

One great advantage of group therapy is cost. If a single therapist is paid, and the group consists of seven members, the resultant savings are obvious.

Conclusion: Psychotherapies, particularly some of the feeling and group therapies, may seem a bit weird. But they don't involve drugs, electric shock treatment, the brain surgeon's knife or detainment. If they can effectively help people to overcome their problems and live fuller, happier lives, they must be OK.

FIRST AID
Save a life for someone

Think how many lives could be saved if we all knew first aid. Most likely it would be someone close like your spouse's, your child's, your friend's. Accidents are unexpected but they do happen, and if they happen near to you it's likely to be to your near and dear ones. If you know the basic, simple rules of first aid, you might just have that marvellous adventure of saving someone's life, earning yourself a small niche in Heaven. Anyone can learn, and everyone should learn. Take a short course with St John's Ambulance, the Red Cross or local group to learn your ABCD:

A. AIRWAY Opening the victim's airway allows fresh air into the lungs. Remove obstructions from the mouth, place one hand under the neck, and with the other on the forehead tilt the head back. Then push the chin upwards. If the patient is breathing, put him into the **recovery position** – lying on his front, his head to one side, one arm alongside his head, the other stretched out underneath the buttock.

B. BREATHING If the patient is not breathing, you must use the **kiss of life**. Don't worry about infection – it never occurs. Check for obstructions in the mouth. Pinch the patient's

---

FIRST AID FACTS

★ A Canadian lumberjack kept a workmate alive for 24 hours until medical aid arrived. He used the kiss of life plus external chest compression continually for that time.

★ It is a ritual among some primitive peoples to knock out one or more front teeth. This originated as a protection against the more serious effects of lockjaw – the victim could be fed until the disease relented.

★ When dealing with a person who has been electrocuted, it is essential *not* to become a victim yourself. If you can't be sure that the electricity supply is *off*, prod the affected person away with a wooden (or plastic) stick, or kick them away with *rubber*-soled shoes.

★ Grandma's method is best for minor burns – water. Bathe the affected part in cold water for at least 10 minutes. For major burns, cover with a sterile non-fluffy cloth and give water by mouth frequently.

nostrils, take a deep breath and blow hard into his mouth. Watch the chest. When it rises properly, remove your mouth. When the chest falls, repeat the inflation. Give the first four inflations as quickly as possible. If the heart beats normally, continue inflations until natural breathing is restored. Then into the recovery position.

C. CIRCULATION Staunch bleeding and get heart beating. If the heart is not beating, you will have to alternate **external chest compression** with the kiss of life. Place heel of hand on centre of lower half of breastbone. Cover with other hand and lock fingers together. Keep arms straight and vertical. Press down two inches. Repeat 15 times at rate of 80 compressions per minute. (Count one and two and three etc.) Give two kisses of life. Repeat compressions 15 times. Repeat kisses of life. And so on. Check heartbeat every minute, by feeling for neck (carotid) pulse. As soon as heartbeat returns, stop compressions. Continue kisses of life until normal breathing resumes. Put patient into recovery position.

D. DIAL 999 Obviously, your first responsibility is to ensure life. If possible, get someone else to make the call. Make sure you give the operator all details. It's amazing how many people ring the emergency services and forget to say where the emergency is taking place.

Action is all important, but you should also try to keep cool and think carefully. These are the major signs:

1 Lack of breathing or heartbeat. Put your ear to the patient's mouth and listen for breathing. Watch chest for movement. Feel the neck pulse to check for heartbeat.

2 Severe bleeding. This should be obvious. Control with direct pressure on the injury. Indirect pressure may be the only way in certain circumstances, but it should *never* be applied for longer than 15 minutes.

3 Unconsciousness. Again obvious.

Remember, to maintain life the human body needs oxygen. If the brain cells are deprived of oxygen they start to die after only three minutes. Effective application of ABC will get blood to the organs, and prevent brain damage or death.

There's more to First Aid than can be squeezed into these two pages. But learning these rules will help. Try out the methods on your friends and family. Learn *practically* how to move the head, feel the breastbone and shift the patient into the recovery position.

But first contact:

- St John Ambulance, 1 Grosvenor Crescent, London, SW1
- St Andrew's Ambulance Assoc., St Andrew's House, Milton Street, Glasgow
- The British Red Cross Society, 9 Grosvenor Crescent, London SW1

For local branches, see the telephone directory.

67

ACUPUNCTURE
Channelling the life force

Have you ever wondered why you feel good after a long walk through the park, away from man-made environment? The Chinese believe this well-being comes from being closer to the forces of nature; that we are all linked by a force common to living things.

This force – called *chi* – is present in the human body as dual flows of energy. These flows, yin and yang, must be in balance in the body and in the universe for us to remain healthy. If there is imbalance for whatever reason, then illness results.

This *chi* life-force runs through the body along set pathways or meridians, moving through the vital organs. If its passage is hindered, illness is the result. Balance can be restored by stimulation of certain points along the main meridians, stimulation effected by the insertion of needles. The qualified acupuncturist knows of 600 points that can be pierced for treatment.

But acupuncture is not just a cure-all, an ancient alternative

---

POINTS AND POINTERS

★ In old China acupuncturists were paid only as long as their patients remained healthy. They were not allowed to examine corpses, so theories about the internal workings of the body were pure guesswork!

★ China has 1,000,000 practitioners. The skilful acupuncturist is able to detect six separate pulses on each wrist, each corresponding to a vital organ.

★ Acupuncture is used in China as a general anaesthetic.

★ Tennis star Ivan Lendl used acupuncture to treat a chronic hip complaint. His decision to rest as well was wise, since acupuncture cannot cure a condition caused by a deliberate stressful imbalance in your lifestyle – in Lendl's case relentless practice and match-play.

★ The insertion of needles in the body results in the production of morphine-like endorphins that act as pain-killers; hence some addicts feel no need to go back on drugs for days after acupuncture treatment!

★ Chinese soldiers used to press a special point below the knee to march further – it was called the 'Three Mile Point' as this was the extra distance covered.

Related arts of healing

★ The related art of acupressure is often used to relieve tension: pressing the fleshy area on the back of the hand between thumb and forefinger can ease headaches.

★ Moxibustion, another related treatment, involves burning herbs directly about the injured area.

★ For combating addiction, studs are placed in the earlobes for the patient to manipulate if sudden craving is experienced.

★ Useful addresses:

The British Acupuncture Association, 34 Alderney Street, London SW1V 4EU. (£1.50 for list of qualified practitioners nationwide.)

The British Medical Acupuncture Society, 67–69 Chancery Lane, London WC2A 1AF. (Provides list of GPs who also practise acupuncture.)

to modern Western medicine. It also reflects an attitude often lacking in modern medicine. A trained acupuncturist will not only be concerned with the outward manifestation of illness – the pain, swelling or rash – but with the underlying cause. That is why on your first visit, a practitioner will ask all sorts of questions, many seeming to have no relation to what's troubling you. The trained practitioner aims to balance the emotional and physical. To do this she must know as much as possible about her patient – personality, emotional state, medical history, indeed anything that might help in discovering and treating the root cause of the illness.

This is why acupuncture is used as a treatment for addictions – smoking, drinking or even eating. The outward manifestation of the addiction – the drink, the cigarette – is the crutch that often helps the person cope with everyday life. But what the acupuncturist hopes to find out is what is making this person so reliant on this particular prop. By sorting out the deep-rooted problems, success is often achieved and the addiction conquered. No acupuncturist claims it's easy; the patient must genuinely want to give up, otherwise treatment is ineffective.

Today, with more of us asking our doctors for help in dealing with the stresses of modern life, we are becoming more dependent on habit-forming drugs. Acupuncture does not guarantee a solution to the problems we face, but it does allow a relaxed view of these problems. The insertion of a needle is but a means to an end – the aim is harmony and balance in the body, and in the world around us.

IMMUNITY
Strategic internal defence system

The human immune system is a wonderfully subtle, complex and sensitive entity (which is probably why it can so easily go wrong). It can be likened to the defence forces of a nation, fighting off dangerous invaders, occasionally mistaking friends for enemies, and turning against itself. It was virtually the only natural defence system we humans possessed until the development of civilization, with its scientific benefits of sewerage, plumbing, regular bathing, methodical nutrition, vaccination and antibiotics. (And Star Wars.)

An understanding of immunity is important, particularly for those hoping to extend their lifespans. Indeed, one of the major theories of the ageing process is based on the concept of **auto-immunity**. This theory argues that, as we get older, our immune systems fail to distinguish between ourselves and our natural

---

IMMUNE REACTIONS

★ Different species are susceptible to different organisms. Rats generally do not get diphtheria and dogs don't get colds.

★ Different strains of the same species similarly vary in their susceptibility. American Indians seem to contract TB more easily than whites.

★ Individuals, even within the same family, also vary in susceptibility and immune competence.

★ Sebaceous secretions and sweat of the skin contain fatty acids that kill bacteria and fungi. The feet, however, are deficient in sebaceous glands, which probably explains their susceptibility to fungal infections such as athlete's foot.

★ There are basically two types of immunity in man: *humoral*, which includes proteins such as immunoglobulin, and *cellular*, different kinds of white blood cell. AIDS occurs when certain white blood cells are attacked by Human Immuno-deficiency Viruses (see Way 78).

★ The immune response is a learning process. After the first contact with an antigen, the white cells retain a memory, and learn skills to deal with the invader.

---

enemies – bacteria, viruses, parasites and other organisms. Certainly, diseases of later life, such as rheumatoid arthritis, thyroid disease and diabetes, are thought to have an auto-immune basis.

The first thing to do is to investigate your family history. Immunity, just like other features, such as height, weight, hair and skin colour, is passed on from generation to generation. If your grandmother was allergic to strawberries, then it shouldn't be too surprising if you're allergic to chocolate. Both allergies, though not identical, indicate a genetic tendency towards a minor immune dysfunction. It may turn out that your daughter is allergic to cats . . . and so on down the line.

Similarly, a family may well be susceptible to diabetes or schizophrenia; knowledge of this can help you take preventive measures before the thing gets out of hand. I would emphasize that the genetic element is so important that a good knowledge of family tendencies, and a wise consideration of their meaning, may be the most useful steps you can take, not just in matters of immunity, but in all areas of health.

Think about your own experience. When you're feeling rough with a cold, remember that it's your immune system going about its normal business. Streaming noses, catarrh and inflammation are part of the process of ridding the body of virus. As many know, hay fever is quite a similar ordeal. In this case, the antigen (the thing that stimulates the immune response) is not a virus – it's pollen! But the response, the driving out of the invader, is not much different.

Similarly, doctors have noticed that environmental pollutants can spark off asthma, although the asthma is actually induced by, for instance, cat dandruff. This is called the 'knock-on effect'. Sensitivity to one thing makes you sensitive to another, and so on and so on, like dominoes.

From a practical point of view, the best thing to do may be to roll with the punches. This is what our grandmothers taught us: if you're feeling ill, get to bed. Relax as much as you can, and let your immune system do the fighting. A bland but nutritious diet, in modest quantities, is necessary to maintain strength. On the other hand, they say a curry is marvellous for a cold . . . work that one out, if you can.

Check for allergies, and extract yourself from the stresses and pollutants of twentieth-century life. In the old days, ill people often escaped to Swiss sanatoria (if they could afford it). As many of them survived serious illnesses, such as tuberculosis, it may be that the treatment was quite effective. Certainly, clean air and restful conditions, coupled with a decent amount of exercise when you're past the worst, must always be a great help to recovery.

133

PRVATE MEDICINE
Liberty hall for some

The poor die earlier than the rich. A Health Education Council report published in 1987, called *The Health Divide*, says the health gap between rich and poor has been growing during the 1980s. The lives of 20,000 a year could be saved, it claims if Britain followed initiatives urged by the World Health Organization.

Those at the bottom of the social scale certainly have higher death rates than those at the top, at every stage of life from birth to old age. This is so even in a country such as ours lucky enough to have a national medical service. Partly, in fact, it's because a private medicine system for the rich exists beside the NHS, even inside it and poaching some of its facilities. It's all right for some! . . . for the patients who can pay extra, and the doctors who can earn extra.

What of using private medicine to keep your own death rate down? Whether it's the socially decent thing to do or not, will it help that much, and can you afford it? Is it really so speedy and efficient, and carried out in such pleasant surroundings? These are some findings by the *Which?* publication, *Self Health*:

Q. Will I get faster treatment?
A. Not if it's urgent. Otherwise, probably yes.
Q. Will I get better treatment?
A. Unlikely.
Q. What about other benefits?
A. You may get more choice and privacy.

The cost of the extra benefits, including the privacy, is high, quite naturally. Specialist consultations can go up to £50, hospital charges in NHS hospitals up to £200 a day and even higher in top private hospitals.

The very rich can afford to pay out themselves. The moderately well-off, about two-thirds of those using private medicine, choose insurance schemes. Many executives are lucky enough to have the premiums put up by their companies, but for others the cost can approach £1000 a year per family.

Then there's the 'small print'. Insurance doesn't cover all the services available under the NHS, or routine treatment from dentists and opticians, or pregnancy and childbirth, geriatric care in hospital, alternative therapies or cosmetic surgery.

If you decide you want private medicine, and plan insuring for it, *Self Health* offers a 'Best Buy Guide' to the fifteen or so agencies on the market. Worth looking at, for some of the charges are startlingly different.

TRANSPLANTS
Making a new person of yourself

Next time you're in for a new heart, why not try a complete new outfit? Yes, it's begun to sneak up on us as real, the old science-fiction fancy that we can wheel a replacement body in under our old head and start up from scratch again.

Triple transplants into heart, lung and liver patients are already the vogue, while donor bodies are now having as many as eight different parts re-used.

Methods are improving all the time, new organs are being tackled. It's clearly worthwhile staying alive another couple of decades, to be around when they finally start giving out long-life season tickets.

Rather be on the receiving than the donor end, certainly – nevertheless it would be doing a good turn to society to make available your own body in the event of death. Think of yourself living on as the essential heart, kidney, liver and cornea in several other humans rather than dying out altogether. Join the 2,000,000 who already have a donor card – just in case.

As well as human parts, we are now using artificial and animal parts, the probable growth area for the future. Hip and other joint replacements are already made from inorganic materials, as are blood vessels. When even muscles and bone, blood and fat are manufactured there will only be left the job of creating an artificial brain. The moment that is done you may not even need to keep your head and fit a new body – there could be a whole new you.

FUTURE PERFECT

★ Kidney transplants are now successful in 80 per cent of cases.

★ Eric McCalla, Birchfield Harriers athlete, missed the 1986 season due to a kidney transplant. He came back in 1987 to a second place triple-jump in the British indoor championships.

★ Soviet geneticists have successfully implanted human brain tissue into rabbits.

★ Material for artificial hearts is capable of flexing 50 million times a year.

★ Mark Howell had a cancerous bone in his leg replaced with metal.

WAYS

71~80

THE MAIN MORTAL ENEMIES

Whatever your fears or nightmares the simple statistical fact is that you are most likely to die from one of three causes: heart disease, cerebrovascular disease (stroke) or cancer. Assuming we don't all go up in a puff of nuclear smoke!

The plain truth is that these three big killers (and even the fourth) are in great part preventable. The adoption of sensible habits, the rejection of stupid ones and the cultivation of sane and civilized attitudes can, without doubt, grace you with many years of cheerful life. Clean air, good food, regular exercise and calmness – these are the simple keys to health.

Attention to your circulation is probably the most important thing of all, for unhealthy arteries will readily clog up and rupture. Even if you've had the misfortune of a heart attack or stroke, the prospects of long-term survival can be bright, as long as you follow your doctor's advice, keep fit with exercise and use your own good sense.

Cancer is less well understood than cardiovascular disease, with one big exception: bronchial carcinoma – and we all know what causes that. But research proceeds, and it's looking like the common sense approach should yield benefit. Brain tumours, for instance, are often secondary to cancers of the lung and liver; and it may be that breast cancer, the bane of the fair sex, is caused in part by stress and bad diet.

Lurking on the horizon is that modern terror AIDS – make sure you don't contract the causative virus. Still in there is our old friend pneumonia, but scientific therapeutic methods may soon dispel its familiar fears. As always, a good general level of health is the best protection against disease.

Protection against nuclear war is another matter – prevention is the only cure in this case. Similarly, avoidance of poisoning, chronic and acute, must be preferable, despite the ever-hopeful possibilities of cure.

71

POISONS
Poisoning, acute and chronic

Acute poisoning causes 3500 deaths a year in Britain, and 100,000 hospital admissions – 15 per cent of all admissions to acute medical units.

You can divide acute poisoning into three categories:

1 Children. You can't blame the little beggars; they know not what they do. The main thing is to keep poisonous substances well out of the way. Lock up cleaning fluids, weedkillers and medicines. For some reason people like to keep medicines in the bathroom, as though they perform a cleansing function, or in food cupboards, for regular daily scoffing. Lock all potential poisons in a single cupboard.

2 Adults. This category accidentally poisons itself by keeping toxic substances in food containers; by failing to read labels; by incorrectly handling dangerous chemicals; from food; and from allergic reactions. Keep your eyes peeled, take care with acids, alkalis, chlorines, petrol and garden chemicals.

3 Suicides and parasuicides (previously called attempted suicides). Groups at particular risk include ages 15–25, over 65s – and doctors.

When dealing with a case of poisoning, Rule One is: ACT FAST. If in any doubt, get the patient to hospital as soon as possible. Phone for an ambulance or, if you have a car and someone who can help you, drive straight to casualty.

Rule Two: try to establish what the poison is, and how much has been consumed. This will help the hospital staff. Take empty containers along to the hospital, to play safe.

The first reaction is often to try to make the patient sick. With some poisons – battery acid or bleach, for instance – this can in fact be dangerous, so it is best to seek professional help without delay.

For poisons in the eye, wash the eye thoroughly with water for 15 minutes. For inhaled poisons, get into fresh air immediately.

Chronic poisoning

This subject is as wide and varied as acute poisoning. Indeed, some chronic poisons, such as nuclear radiation, lead and other environmental pollutants, may pose a more serious threat to the general health of the population. These are a source of continual research and debate.

BRAIN TUMOURS
A chance of being saved

Among the more enigmatic of cancers is the tumour of the brain, precisely because it affects the brain. Its interference with neighbouring brain tissue gives it the uncanny power of producing symptoms in other organs far removed from the tumour itself, by sending signals from the brain through the nervous system.

The symptoms could be deafness, or partial loss of sight or weakness of the body on one side. These develop because the tumour, even when of benign nature, grows steadily larger inside the confined space of the skull – until it compresses or destroys that area of the brain that controls the particular function.

Sometimes the expanding tumour presses forcefully on the skull itself. This can then lead to more localized symptoms, such as terrible headaches. It can also bring about mental symptoms that include loss of memory, hallucination and sometimes general deterioration of the intellect.

There are different kinds of tumours that invade the brain, affecting different sets of people; this contributes to the strange distribution of the disease: it is most common in children below ten years of age and in people aged between 50 and 70 . . . and

DISTRIBUTION OF THE DISEASE

★ In an extensive study, some brain tumours were found to be more common in rural than in urban areas.

★ Nearly 25 per cent of all brain tumours are secondary to growths elsewhere, usually in the lung, breast, stomach, prostate, kidney or thyroid. About two-thirds of these had spread from the lungs.

★ Here is a range of symptoms from varied tumours: demented behaviour, headache, convulsions, deafness, depression, speech impairment and enlargement of the extremities of the skeleton – nose, jaws, fingers and toes.

★ Virtually every type of cerebral disease can mimic a brain tumour.

★ Dentists run twice the risk of contracting certain brain tumours, most likely caused by contact with amalgam, chloroform, X-rays.

Newer, better techniques

Operating on a brain tumour clearly requires the most precise and brilliant surgical work, by virtue of the delicate nature of the surrounding tissues. Add to that another requirement; the need to avoid disfiguring the patient. New techniques that don't require the surgeon to go in through the forehead or elsewhere on the skull, leaving visible scars, have been developed in recent years. Some patients now have their tumours attended to through a complicated internal route – in through the mouth, up in front of the top teeth, behind the nose and thence into the front of the skull.

The only opening made, then, is on the site of the upper gums, out of public view. However, to patch this up again with its own special sort of tissue, the surgeon must take his scalpel off to another site, the thigh. There he makes a cut above the patient's knee, digs deep down to the bone and scrapes off spare material of a related type that he finds there.

So the patient in the end has two operations, but the process as a whole is made safer and is less unsightly. And he can claim to have his leg in his head.

more often in males than females.

Slowly over the years the number of brain tumour deaths reported in Britain has been rising. No definite reason has been found for this, except what is not really a reason at all: the fact that more skilful diagnosis is showing up cases that were not recognized as such before.

However, treatment, too, has been improving in recent years, and many patients are cured, while others are given relief or helped to added years of life.

The doctor's first task in deciding on treatment is to make sure that the brain tumour is not simply the secondary of a cancer elsewhere in the body, often lung cancer. In such cases it is mostly not worth applying surgery or other interventions that the surgeons term 'heroic' – calling for a hopeless sacrifice by the patient. After all, sadly, other secondaries could arise as well.

When it is a primary incidence, however, it is worthwhile removing the tumour completely, or applying methods to restrict its growth.

As always the earlier the tumour is spotted the better the chances of treatment; thus the very improvement in diagnosis leads in fact to the saving of lives, whatever the apparent growth statistically.

I ♡ MY HEART
You'd better – it's the only one you've got

Every hour a coachload of people die of cardiovascular disease. That's 1000 a day, yet this creates less of a popular sensation than a pile-up on the motorways.

And many of those heart deaths by the coachload are quite avoidable, that's the sadness. Imagine, 1000 lives a day, or 350,000 a year – the population of Southampton – might be saved, with common sense and care, and a certain amount of will-power.

Be warned, it's the disease *you're* most likely to die of yourself – and sooner than you think if you don't take steps now. You can see that taking your heart in hand is as important as all the other 98 ways put together.

What each of us needs if we are to stay alive until 100 is a heart engine that will run continuously for a century. Well, although man has split the atom, been to the moon and back and created the microchip revolution, he is yet to invent a pump to match the human heart-engine in this requirement. So we must devote

---

HEART FRAGMENTS

★ One half of all deaths in most Western countries are caused by atherosclerosis – the furring up of the arteries with atheroma.

★ The heart pumps 5000 gallons of blood per day – enough in a lifetime to fill the Albert Hall.

★ There are 30,000 miles of arteries in the body.

★ A quarter of the male population of Britain will suffer a heart attack before the age of 65.

★ The heart is not the largest or heaviest organ in the body. That distinction goes to the liver.

★ Despite their high consumption of bear and seal meat, Eskimos have little heart disease. This has been attributed to their high intake of fish.

★ Some doctors claim it is possible to restart your own heart after an attack by coughing sharply a number of times.

★ Dr Abe Davis of Cape Town is a dextrocardiac. His heart is on the right side of his body . . . he's still alive and well at 86.

ourselves to maintaining our own hearts free of disease; there is nothing good enough in the way of spare parts for us to rely on. By the turn of the century there may be plenty in stock, but can you be sure of hanging on meanwhile?

Generally speaking heart disease is not a condition of the heart itself but of the circulatory system that depends on the heart and, reciprocally, upon which the heart depends. It is the general clogging-up of the arteries leading to and from the heart that causes one-half of the total deaths in our affluent society. This clogging up is responsible for 80 per cent of all heart disease, including heart attack, angina, thrombosis – and also stroke.

There are several factors that predispose people to heart problems, some of them that can be corrected, such as obesity, and some that cannot, such as the genetic pattern you inherit, which you can work out from your parents' own longevity . . . but it's notable that even then you can do enough by regular exercise to offset any handicap of birth. (If they died from heart attacks and died young, you're at extra risk.)

Here are *five* simple things you can do to give yourself years of extra life:

1 Exercise
Fit people have fewer heart attacks. The heart is a muscle, and like all muscles gets stronger from exercise. It gets its particular form of exercise from pumping blood around the body when the body is doing vigorous work. All you need are three 20-minute sessions of vigorous exercise a week – a total of *one hour*.

2 Stop smoking
Cigs kill in more ways than one. They thicken the blood, damage the cells called platelets, cause clotting and weaken the heart. Most doctors have now stopped smoking; as a result their own heart disease rate has plummeted. Be your own doctor and save your own life. Give up now and your chances of heart attack will dramatically decrease.

3 Check blood pressure
As many as one in ten of over-45 year olds have high blood pressure. Your doctor can diagnose and treat this quite easily. If you have severe hypertension, start up an exercise programme, *gently*.

4 Beware of fat
On your body rather than on your plate. Obesity is a severe risk factor in CVD, as well as depressing the sex drive, and predisposes you to diabetes and its dangers of kidney failure and blindness. Cut down on your eating.

5 Relax
Some authorities believe that stress is the most important cause of twentieth-century illness. Serious crises, such as bereavement and divorce, are acknowledged life-shorteners. Try meditation, counselling, massage, deep breathing, ear plugs and catnaps.

141

74

BREAST CANCER
A better outlook today

Treatment of breast cancer is improving all the time. It is still a serious disease, the chief cancer among women, but the recovery rate is far better than for, say, lung cancer.

These are some factors that predispose a woman, if only slightly, towards contracting breast cancer:

★ A history of benign breast disease.
★ A family history of breast cancer, especially in a close relative such as mother, sister or aunt.
★ Childlessness or late motherhood.
★ A long menstrual history, of 35 years or more.
★ A history of other cancers, especially of the uterus, ovary or colon.

The most important thing to do to improve your survival rate is regular **breast self-examination** (BSE). Early diagnosis reduces mortality by half. At the very least it means treatment will be less traumatic.

Remember: BSE every month, either a few days after periods, or on the first day of the month. Women over 40 should also join

---

MORE THAN HALF SURVIVE

★ In the UK alone more than 30,000 women a year develop breast cancer.

★ The following are not numbered among the causes: a knock, blow or bite on the breast, fondling, breast-feeding, sunbeds or topless sun-bathing or an active sex life.

★ Some research indicates that vegetarians have a lower incidence of the disease.

★ The radiation risk of mammography is no greater than from one-third of a cigarette.

★ High fat consumption has been linked to breast cancer.

★ Five years after they were treated in 1978, 61 per cent of patients were still alive.

★ Women who start menstruating late seem to have a lower rate of the disease. Too much food seems to be a factor . . . by not overfeeding your daughters you may protect them.

Post operatively . . .

If you are diagnosed as having breast cancer you may well have to undergo a mastectomy or combination of lump removal with radiotherapy and other therapies. Don't underestimate the psychological and sexual effects of such an operation. It may take you some time to recover; join a self-help group.

Nevertheless you should be able to carry on an absolutely normal life. Barbara, an orchestral musician, had both breasts removed. After convalescence she returned to her internationally famous orchestra and is fiddling away to this day, well past retirement age.

an annual screening programme through their doctor or Community Health Council.

Interestingly, it is often the husband or boyfriend who spots the ominous lump.

This is how you do it yourself:

1 Buy a notebook to record your monthly BSE and compare, month by month.
2 Stand before a mirror, undressed to the waist and arms to the side. Look carefully at your breasts, turning from side to side; look underneath them as well.
3 Raise your arms above your head, and examine the upper part of the breast that leads to the armpit.
4 With hands on hips, press inwards until your chest muscles tighten, looking for any skin dimpling.
5 Lean forward and examine each breast in turn. Is there any puckering, or unusual change in outline?

(Do the next two steps either lying down, or in the bath, where soapy fingers will make it easier):

6 First examine your left breast with the right hand (feel with the flat pads of the middle three fingers; press towards the chest wall, using firm but gentle pressure). Systematically cover the whole breast, the armpit and the top of the collar bone.
7 Slide your hand over your left nipple, looking for any discharge, puckering or retraction. Repeat for the right breast.

You'll be looking for any unusual lumps or changes in shape, puckering of the skin, a swelling in the upper arm or, of course, any pain or discomfort not felt before.

If you do find what appears to be a lump, mark it with a felt-tip pen and show it to your GP. Most lumps are not serious, but delaying through fear could prevent something serious from being spotted early.

75

LUNG CANCER
The cancer we can stop

Some of the best and brightest have been victims of this dreadful and unnecessary disease. Pat Phoenix, Nat 'King' Cole, George VI, Buster Keaton and Duke Ellington – all cut down by the Devil, Tobacco. Money won't help you, neither fame or beauty. A few, a very few, may survive, but for the vast majority life will end in hellish pain.

Lung cancer patients have a 5 per cent survival rate: 1 in 20 – poor odds indeed. Many a patient is subjected to ghastly surgery, sickening chemotherapy and radiotherapy, yet still drops dead after a few weeks. Not a pleasant prospect.

The good news is that it's almost completely preventable. Any fool, with just a pinch of will-power, can escape this unenviable fate. A few days of uncomfortable craving is a cheap price to pay for another 20 years of life. The death rate from lung

---

FIRST, THE BAD NEWS

★ Scotland holds the world record for lung cancer; the rate is 71 per 100,000.

★ Death from lung cancer can be particularly unpleasant. Some patients literally choke to death.

★ Ionizing radiations can also cause lung cancer (though cigarettes are responsible for by far the greatest number of cases). Uranium miners in Colorado, and other miners of radioactive ores, have a high death rate from the disease.

★ Don't think lung cancer just affects your lungs. It commonly spreads to the brain, the bones, the liver, the lymph nodes and other sites, causing considerable agony.

★ If you've given up smoking for ten years or more, your chances of getting lung cancer are no greater than those of non-smokers.

★ There has been much recent research into passive smoking – the effects of inhaling other people's cigarette smoke. Don't give lung cancer to your friends, family and children.

cancer for heavy smokers is *forty* times, that's *forty* times, greater than for non-smokers.

Two other lung poisons to avoid are asbestos and atmospheric pollution. Urban dwellers and asbestosis sufferers both have higher mortality rates.

But the Number One cause, as first proved by Drs Doll and Peto, is undoubtedly the cigarette. Innocent looking, isn't it? A handy little friend, clad in virginal white with a cute little brown bottom, delivered to you in a handsome packet of red, gold or black. Who would believe that it could cause such lethal misery?

It's not really that difficult to give up. Millions have, with just a little initial discomfort and a few months of self-discipline. Men suffer three times as much as women – more than 50 per cent of all male cancer deaths are from 'bronchial carcinoma'. The offered image may be manly, but a Real Man should be strong enough to cast aside such a nasty and demeaning little habit. Giving up provides more money for booze, romance, rugby boots and skiing holidays. A note for the ladies: don't get smug – your cancer rate is increasing all the time, as the long-term effects of female smoking accumulate.

Many cures for smoking have been tried, with varying success. My advice is to try them all, one by one, and keep on trying until you reach the goal.

1 Taking up exercise is a wonderful antidote: it's not too easy to swim or run and smoke at the same time, and as your enthusiasm for your sport grows so your reliance on cigarettes will wane.

2 Nicotine chewing gum (Nicorette). About 20 per cent success rate. Costs less than cigarettes, though still hurts the pockets of the poor. Should be available free, but the government is strangely reluctant.

3 Acupuncture. 15 per cent success rate. Costs vary, and so do practitioners. If you don't succeed with one, try another.

4 Hypnosis. No figures available. Can be used in conjunction with acupuncture. Some good reports.

5 Tobacco repellent tablets. No figures. Some good reports. Quite cheap.

6 Psychotherapy. May work, but many therapists are smokers.

7 Cigars and pipes. Some people switch from cigarettes to these, which they then find easier to give up. Roundabout way of doing it, but if it works, it works. Good cigars cost a fortune. Risk of cancers of lip, mouth and oesophagus.

8 Dietary change. People who become vegetarians will often give up smoking quite easily.

9 Emotional shock. The death of a friend or family member will frequently induce a person to give up. Just imagine if that dead person was *you*.

76

BLOOD PRESSURE
A weakness of the flesh

Hypertension – high blood pressure – is not only a disease in itself, it's a cause of other diseases. It's an augury of strokes and coronaries.

Once into the thirties heart disease is already a serious threat, and with the possibility that blood pressure is lurking in the background, this is something that must be checked for in any adult, then tackled forthwith. The most important thing is avoidance.

Here's your avoidance plan: first be clear about the under-

HIGH PRESSURE APPROACH

★ One-third of all heart attacks happen between 30 and 45 years of age, almost all in smokers.

★ More than 1,500,000 Britons have blood pressure well above the average.

★ Those with hypertension have five times the heart failure rate and seven times the stroke rate of the normal person.

★ Two blood-pressure drugs that cost the Health Service £120,000,000 a year helped only about one patient in 1000 – a finding by the Medical Research Council. What's more the drugs were responsible for serious side effects. As many as 20 per cent of the guinea pigs used in the research had to withdraw during the drug-taking programme due to such effects as impotence in men, gout, diabetes, dizziness and nausea.

★ The big salt controversy 1: 'Although more moderate salt restriction does seem to reduce blood pressure when it is very high or moderately high, the evidence for a beneficial effect in people with very mild blood pressure is conflicting.' (*Which?* magazine)

★ The big salt controversy 2: Almost all the salt in our diet is already present in the food we eat, as much as 36 per cent of it in cereal products; whereas as little as 12 per cent of our intake is from salt added in cooking or at table. Thus there is little opportunity for cutting back salt without radical diet changes; a pinch or two at table is hardly significant.

---

lying causes, so that you understand what to avoid. For you can control those causes. After all, blood pressure does not arrive from above, in a little package with your name on it . . . it is something you have earned for yourself. With your obliging help the damage has gone on working away silently over the years. So, a further thought: even those in their twenties have to sit up and take notice.

The major causes are stress, obesity, smoking and sedentary living, those very weaknesses of the flesh found under so many of the 99 headings. They're mostly interlinked, too; smoking adds to stress, sedentary living causes obesity, and then obesity makes it so much harder to take up an active style again – Catch 22! Another item also figuring on many black lists is parental history, though there's no reason to despair if your parents or siblings were victims, because taking up the recommended treatment will improve your chances, anyway.

Step No. 1, then: crack down on the causes – and right away! Slow up in the rat race, keep the weight in check, make sure to throw out the cigarettes and move to a regular light exercise regime.

Step No. 2: a medical check-up. Mostly you don't even know hypertension's there until it's been measured . . . the silent delinquent! A check-up is no big task for your doctor. Ask for it. If it does come up that your blood pressure is higher than it should be for your age, the doctor will offer you advice, to which you will need to give full attention. Depending on the degree of hypertension, ways will be suggested for combating it; you may be prescribed tablets, or advised to cut out salt or to make other dietary changes.

Until this last year or so there was a great deal of uncertainty about some of these remedies. Controversy still surrounds the low-fat dietary advice, while the low-salt school recently received an emphatic negative vote from a weighty group of British medical authorities. But now something positive has emerged from another scientific study, by a research team in Australia, and published in *The Lancet*. The results are solid and significant – and helpful: they point to action that can actually be taken by anyone who is suffering from high blood pressure.

The Australians found that regular light exercise clearly reduced blood pressure in their patients – here's the really important point – and that the reduction was 'considerably greater than observed after dietary methods such as reduced salt intake or vegetarianism'.

Of course exercise had already achieved general approval as the best method of *avoiding* blood pressure; now it's voted the right thing to do both before and after. You're on to a big win against nothing with exercise; start your jogging or fitness walking project today.

PNEUMONIA
The old people's killer

77

Pneumonia! – not so long ago, the very word struck fear. Before antibiotics, it was responsible for great mortality. It was a disease of intense drama, patients suffering a week of fever and delirium before a 'crisis' was reached; at which point their fate was determined: either the fever broke, to be followed by a slow resolution and recovery, or they died. One in four used to die, either from the disease itself or complications such as pleurisy or heart failure.

The main victims were the aged. Some even dubbed it 'the old people's friend', as it released the weak and infirm through a gentle death. It is still today a common ending to many illnesses in old age, producing the characteristic 'death rattle'.

Pneumonia is an inflammatory condition of the lung, the air sacs become so filled with fluid as a result of infection that breathing is impaired. As recovery takes place, the fluid is coughed up. Pneumonia can involve one or more lobes of the lungs (lobar pneumonia), or patches of both lungs in different areas (bilateral or double pneumonia).

Many organisms cause it, among them bacteria, viruses and fungi. Virus pneumonia tends to attack young people, runs its course in about ten days, and leaves its victim weak and

DID YOU KNOW?

★ If you've had pneumonia before, you're more susceptible to attack.

★ Pregnant women with flu are more likely to develop pneumonia than women not pregnant.

★ Twice as many women as men die from pneumonia. (Twice as many men as women die from bronchitis.)

★ The incidence of pnuemonia and bronchitis among children where even one parent smokes is *double*.

★ Anything that restricts movement of the chest, even the simple strapping of a fractured rib, is an invitation for bronchopneumonia to develop.

★ Winona Mildred Melick, born 1876, survived four major cancer operations (in 1918, 1933, 1966 and 1968) only to succumb to pneumonia in December 1981, when 105.

Avoiding pneumonia

Keep the lungs working away; even when ill stay as active as possible. Remember that movement is life. When bed-ridden:

Move about in bed as much as possible, changing position if you wake at night. Keep bedclothes loose to encourage movement.

Sit in bed with head and neck well-supported (tuck a small, sausage-shaped pillow behind your neck) to help fluid in the chest drain away.

Try exercises in bed. For a full two minutes at a time, bend the knees, roll the legs, point the toes, stretch the spine. And add breathing exercises.

debilitated for a while. Bronchopneumonia attacks older, bedridden people, where circulation is sluggish. It is the main reason for a higher mortality rate in geriatric wards between January and April every year, due to higher cold-weather admissions. (All the more reason to keep old people out of hospital and at home!)

Bronchopneumonia can also be caused by food going down the wrong way and becoming trapped; inhaling irritating chemicals such as liquid paraffin, kerosene and petrol; or as a complication from another disease.

Bacterial pneumonia is most often caused by germs present in healthy mouths and throats; the commonest way to get it is from an infection spreading down the bronchial tubes due to bronchitis.

Pneumonia can come when the body's resistance is low – so anyone can develop it, from the newborn baby to the 80-year-old bedridden invalid. Those at greatest risk are the elderly, the immobile, the undernourished, the overweight, smokers, and those with other diseases such as diabetes. Among young and middle-aged adults, excessive drinkers are particularly suscep-tible: it is the greatest health risk in DTs, where the victim hallucinates.

The striking thing about early pneumonia is that the symptoms don't point to the lungs: the patient has a headache rather than a chest pain, and feels very unwell, although with no idea of what's wrong. After a few hours, however, a harsh, dry cough and pain on breathing make the diagnosis clear, accom-panied by shivering, fever and a rapid pulse rate. Rust-coloured sputum is brought up, and when tapping the patient's chest a GP hears dull thuds rather than the hollow sound given off by healthy lungs.

AIDS
. . . Be careful!

There is no doubt that AIDS (acquired immune deficiency syndrome) is a very serious problem. However, it is by no means the first major epidemic to afflict mankind: smallpox, syphilis, bubonic plague and even measles have killed millions in the past. All were frightening, insoluble mysteries at first. These have all been dealt with, and it is safe to predict that AIDS, with our modern medical knowledge, *will* be conquered. Panic helps nobody. The best remedy at the moment, apart from massive investment in research and education, is sensible caution and general good health. Medical journals report that 'immune competence', which is a result of good health, can prevent infection – and can prevent progression towards serious disease.

The first step is to avoid infection:

1. It seems that *monogamy* is the safest bet – but you must be sure that your partner is monogamous too. This may present

---

KNOWLEDGE IS POWER

★ In America the rate of increase in the number of AIDS cases is falling. The 'doubling time', the time it takes for the number of cases to double, has fallen from 9 months to 13 months.

★ A recent study of German prostitutes, who use condoms at all times, has shown that *none* was infected with the offending virus.

★ In New York City in 1986, AIDS killed a total of 2139 people.

★ One of the drugs that may be useful in treatment of AIDS, called AZT, is made from herring sperm.

★ Much of the spread of AIDS in Africa, according to the *British Medical Journal*, is due to blood transfusion. African hospitals are unable to afford a comprehensive screening programme. Perhaps the rich nations can help here? It would, in the long run, be to all our benefit.

★ Theories of the origin of AIDS abound: from outer space, from a messed-up experiment, from the CIA, from the KGB . . . One authority has even suggested that it was acquired from monkeys, possibly by eating them.

problems for the single or those who are widowed, divorced or separated.

2. *Safer sex* is being counselled. This involves the use of sturdy condoms, the non-entrance of semen or blood into bodies, abstinence during menstruation, avoidance of oral and anal sex.

3. *No needle-sharing*. Of course, it's much better not to take intravenous drugs at all, but if you can't stop, make absolutely sure you use a clean needle every time. Your doctor may oblige.

4. *General good health*. See above.

If you have a test and are 'antibody-positive', remember it is by no means a death sentence. There are three states of infectivity:

Positivity. This state is symptomless. It simply means that your body has manufactured antibodies against a Human Immuno-deficiency Virus (HIV). You are, of course, a carrier, and may pass on the virus, or even the disease, to another.

AIDS related complex (ARC). This condition has some of the symptoms of the full-blown disease, but does not seem to progress in the same lethal fashion.

AIDS. The prognosis is not good, it must be admitted. There are signs, though, that patients are not dying as quickly as they once were. This may be for psychological or other reasons. New drugs are constantly being tested, and there are strong hopes for at least two: AZT and HIVA.

There are two major ways of preventing the infection progressing to major disease. These are:

1. Avoidance of re-infection. It may well be that constant re-infection is a major factor in the development of AIDS. *Don't* think that, because you're positive, you can continue to indulge in dangerous behaviour without additional risk.

2. General good health. Try and find a routine that's healthy for you, bearing in mind the advice you'll find in other sections of this book. Life is a series of risks, keep them to a minimum.

It is worth repeating that medical science is capable of quite remarkable results. However, equipment and labour cost money. One of the best health measures you can take is to pressure governments, businesses, charities and other organizations to put more money into research.

If you're at all worried, and even if you're not, but you think you ought to be, go and see your doctor.

As this book goes to press, a number of new and exciting developments have been announced in AIDS research. Perhaps the most important is the discovery of a factor, Gc2, which some people have in their systems, and which seems to prevent infection. The biochemistry is extremely complex, but the news brings help and inspiration to researchers.

CEREBROVASCULAR DISEASE
Life after stroke

Handel wrote 'The Messiah' four years after a stroke. Pasteur successfully developed immunization against anthrax and rabies with his left side paralysed by stroke. And there are countless other cases, great and humble, of lives continuing successfully after stroke. With patience and help from friends, relatives and medics, and with determination and wisdom drawn from within themselves, stroke patients have much to offer and much to look forward to.

But prevention must be the first step. A stroke is no party, and effective prevention is possible.

The main preventive measures are much the same as for heart disease. The process of **atherosclerosis** is the underlying cause of both stroke and heart disease. Atherosclerosis simply means the narrowing and hardening of the arteries, and it is caused by the gradual building up of atheroma in the arteries. This is often likened to the 'furring' of water pipes in a house's plumbing.

Put simply, the furring-up of the heart's arteries leads to heart attack; the furring-up of the brain's arteries leads to stroke. Keep your arteries clear, and you'll vastly increase your chances of escaping these major killers.

It is vigorous activity – through aerobic exercise! – that will help to keep the brain's arteries clear just as well as those of the heart. Humanity was never built for lying around and over-indulging . . . yes, some of the time, but not all year round. We need frequent exercising of our parts to keep them in trim. Probably, heavy bouts of mental exercise too would be beneficial in the case of the brain. (See suggestions in Pointers to self-action.)

Recovery from stroke can be slow and difficult, but as Handel and Pasteur have shown it can be marvellously productive. Rehabilitation these days is usually carried out by a team consisting of doctors, nurses, physiotherapists, occupational therapists and speech therapists. Each of these specialists has undergone lengthy and rigorous training, so follow their instructions, no matter how depressed or useless you may be feeling.

The first few days or weeks after a stroke can be particularly difficult, and at least 70 per cent of patients become depressed. So don't be surprised if you feel down. And this is when you should remember too that the most important member of the team will be yourself, for the more effort that you put in the more the chance of success.

Complete recovery from a stroke is possible, although it

Pointers to self action

★ Keep your blood pressure *low*. Get it checked regularly. Remember, high blood pressure is often quite symptomless, and it is the biggest risk factor for stroke.

★ Stop smoking. At the very least, smoking damages your heart – and a weak heart is an important risk factor for stroke.

★ Take other measures to strengthen your heart. Exercise regularly. Learn to breathe and relax.

★ Check for diabetes. Diabetes, high blood pressure and high levels of fats in the blood (which tend towards atherosclerosis) are all linked. Good control of diabetes will knock another few points off your stroke risk table.

★ Watch for Transient Ischaemic Attacks (TIAs). These are mini-strokes, usually lasting for no more than a few minutes. A person who has had a TIA is at much greater risk of suffering a full stroke. Loss of vision in one eye, disturbances of movement or sensation are common symptoms. Check with your GP.

★ Avoid stress. If you can't avoid it, learn how to cope with it. It seems pretty certain that stress increases your chances of heart attack and stroke.

★ Check your family history. Like many things, stroke has a genetic component. If other members of your family have had strokes, it's particularly important to consider their risky behaviour and try and modify your own to improve your own chances.

★ Don't get fat, or if you are already, slim down. Obesity in itself definitely increases the likelihood of diabetes and heart disease – and thereby stroke as well.

★ Some studies show an increased stroke risk in young women taking the oestrogen contraceptive pill. If your other risk factors are high, you might consider alternative contraceptive methods.

depends on the extent of the damage. What you can do is strive religiously to avoid that second or third stroke – the one that might be your last. So prevention is always the key, even if you've already had one. In the 19 years between his first and second strokes, Louis Pasteur probably did as much for humanity as anyone who ever lived.

NUCLEAR WAR
It can seriously damage your health

A full-scale nuclear war would undoubtedly cause more death and destruction than any other event in history. Forget the Black Death, forget the earthquakes and famines – tea parties in comparison. A really big conflict, with missiles and bombers flying all over the place, might well kill more people than all other wars put together. And for the few who survived, the earth would be a miserable hole. If human life could continue (and this is debatable) it would be confined for many years to hellish underground prisons, with paltry provision, no sunlight and precious little pleasure. Many people feel, not unreasonably, that they would rather go quickly. As the man said: 'If it drops, I'll catch it.'

Even a little bomb dropped on, say, Paris would be no picnic. And the bombs that are being set off *now*, on atolls in the South Pacific or underground in the USA, may well be doing permanent damage to the world's delicate ecological balance. The USSR, too, has now resumed tests.

MIGHTY ATOM

★ The Atomic Age began in 1896, when Rutherford and Thomson discovered the electron and Becquerel first described radioactivity. It took a mere 49 years for the modest research programme to result in the first nuclear bomb.

★ The most effective fission bombs work on a process of implosion. Explosives surround a hollow sphere of uranium or plutonium. Detonation squeezes the fission-able fuel into a 'supercritical mass'. Then . . . bang.

★ Many famous atomic scientists, such as Enrico Fermi, Marie Curie and her daughter Irène, died early from cancer or leukaemia, despite winning the Nobel Prize.

★ If you receive a radiation dose of 8000 rads or more, you will certainly die within 48 hours.

★ Spain had a lucky break in 1966. A US B–52 bomber collided into a refuelling tanker in mid-air, and offloaded four atomic bombs in the 20–25 megaton range. The detonation devices went off, causing some contamination, but all four bombs were recovered.

It's all a bit too much to think about. None the less, the problem is there – hiding heads in the sand won't help much. Perhaps, if enough people make themselves fully aware of the problems, we might begin to move towards a nuclear-free world.

There are three possible types of nuclear catastrophe:

1 Superpower conflict. Generally speaking, this is taken to mean a war between America and NATO on the one hand and Russia and the Warsaw Pact on the other.

2 Conflict resulting from proliferation of weapons. France, Britain, Israel, India, China, and probably Pakistan and South Africa now have nuclear weapons. A number of other countries are candidates for the rather dubious 'Nuclear Club'.

3 Nuclear terrorism. The province of the 'amateurs' – it may well be that they could produce a crude bomb, and use it. Even without sophisticated means of delivery, they could wreak havoc on a big city.

What to do about this threat? Short of a fantastical technical invention (some sort of magic vacuum cleaner that sucks up radiation) the answers seem to be primarily political. President Reagan's 'Star Wars' initiative is rather a long shot. Even if the system could successfully protect America from Russia, it would be of no use against terrorism, or in a war between Australia and New Zealand or between Sweden and Norway. Deep in our hearts, we're all aware (Reagan and Gorbachev as much as the next person) that agreement and compromise are the answers. Humanity has to accept the fact that world peace is an evolutionary necessity. But for this to be realized, it would mean:

1 Making the world a less stressful place, and thus lessening incentives to violence. People tend to resort to violence through greed or misery. A satisfied person will not start a war. He's unlikely even to start a fight, unless he's been drinking.

2 Applying pressure on governments to reduce defence spending. The more sophisticated and hi-tech the weapons, the more likelihood of an accident. An accidental nuclear war is just as nasty as an intended one.

3 Positive moves towards world government. Most people are well aware that we live on a single planet. World government, with a jurisdiction over the means of mass destruction, is a natural progression, as we begin, slowly, to colonize other worlds, solar systems and galaxies. Let's hope humanity doesn't do too much damage on Mars.

Nevertheless, be prepared in case of accidental fallout: don't go out in the rain; shower frequently; don't drink milk; avoid contaminated food; take iodine tablets.

WAYS

81~90

SPORT AND TRANSPORT

With the rise in automation we should see a decline in the time spent on work. This may be a difficult change for people, but it will ultimately result in more space for other activities. Foremost among these, no doubt, will be those popular pursuits sport and travel. After all, with improved communications the whole wide world will be open to all: from Tomsk to Trinidad, from Juneau to Djakarta. And when we're at home, what better way to pass an afternoon than a friendly and invigorating game of rounders?

Travel can be risky, as any driver knows. A careful perusal of Way 82 should help you to lessen your risks of death and injury. Stupid drivers continue, despite all the warnings, to slaughter one another (not to mention innocent pedestrians) in their attempts to cut two minutes off a journey. Is it worth it?

Travel abroad brings other risks: plane crashes and boat sinkings take a minor toll. And if you head for the tropics, a thousand formidable creatures await you. Planning ahead, with the proper vaccinations and a handy supply of anti-malarials, could stop your dream holiday from turning into a nightmare. Trips closer to home, to a nearby river for gentle canoeing, or just around the corner for volleyball, contain less risks but no less opportunity for relaxation and fun.

Professional sport can be exciting, but there's nothing as good as doing it yourself, even if it's just a game of bowls. There's no reason why you should be restricted to conventional sports either. Try pelota, if you can find a suitable court, or rugby polo if there's a shallow pool to hand, or American football if you have a hankering to break a leg! There are more than 1000 sports centres throughout the nation, so bad weather need never be a hindrance.

The secret of long life is not simply avoiding illness – positive attitudes and full enjoyment of leisure time are just as essential, for mind, body and soul.

WATER TRAVEL
No messing about with safety!

Sea-faring became the safest as well as the cheapest way to travel last century with the introduction of iron hulls and steam power. Ship owners pushed home the safety benefit hard, at one time commonly adding extra dummy funnels to vessels to give passengers yet more confidence in their power and security.

Yet today how many cross the ocean by liner? Who bothers to compare safety at sea with road or air? Inland transport too – if you choose to chug slowly across the country by barge, you know you need give your safety little thought.

Each year but a few dozen people drown as a result of water transport accidents in Britain. It hardly adds up even if you were to include the number of British lost at sea when travelling abroad.

Nevertheless, it's worth analysing the make-up of those British water transport statistics closely and noting a lesson from them: in 1983, 52 males died this way, and only 3 females; in 1984, 49 and 5. Astonishing, yet year by year the proportion is similar. And the greatest peril comes at summer weekends. What does this all say, very explicitly? That it's water sport, messing around in small boats, we're talking about . . . favoured mostly by men. Not transport for going somewhere, but transport for transport's sake.

Operating in the realm of statistics, we can coolly turn this thought completely on its head, of course. Water sport is in fact rather *dangerous*; it's simply not as frequently undertaken as commuting by train or cycle. Consider canoeing, accountable for less than half a dozen deaths in a year . . . if the whole population of Britain took to their canoes for one afternoon a week we would lose 50,000 of them in a year. Even the frightful car death figure is far lower than that, about a tenth of its incidence. Watersportsmen know the safety rules; it is up to them to be in earnest about observing them.

Still, the message is that on the whole you're safe enough travelling over the water in this country. Beware though if you find yourself aboard one of those passenger ferries in the Far East, which figure regularly in brief news items in the papers: 'More than 280 were drowned when an overcrowded ferry sunk off Djakarta yesterday.'

Just lately, alas, we discovered with the Herald of Free Enterprise disaster that ferries to and from our own country were also vulnerable. The spotlight focused on several other minor ferry incidents, too, in the months after Zeebrugge. All this has helped to stimulate ship designers to further safety efforts and marine authorities to enforce stricter regulations at sea.

MOTOR CARS
The killing roads

Most people have little worry in undertaking a road journey, even gaily submitting to being driven off in an old banger by an accident-prone partygoer on a murky night. Yet oddly enough these same people have a morbid fear of flying in a splendidly maintained airliner piloted by a sober, experienced man. Yet compare these statistical facts: at any moment somewhere in the world 700,000 air passengers are in flight, of whom on average 400 are killed each year. Using the road in Britain, at any moment, are about the same number, 650,000. On average 5500 of them are killed annually – more than ten times those in the air. Add the deaths on the roads in other highly motorized countries and the contrast is a hundred times as grim.

So for safety's sake it appears you should spend all your time in the air rather than on the road – an impossibility. Instead learn the grave warning that the car is a dangerous weapon and vow to keep the safety-catch on. Change your character as a driver. Become meek instead of macho – adopt the philosophy of do-as-you-would-be-done-by.

This is the game to play: give way *every time*, allow the impatient to pass, don't get angry when honked, let yourself be insulted without reprisal, be last away from the light, don't curse the pedestrian, the cyclist, the motor bike, and so . . .
For each of these noble actions award yourself a Good Deed Star, and don't finish any trip without ten stars.

When you've become a thorough saint, you can study and

BLACK SPOTS

★ 25 million have been killed in motor accidents since the car took to the road at the beginning of this century. By 2000 AD the car will have killed more people than both World Wars together – 45–50 million.

★ In Sacramento, California, two motorists were killed in a bumper-to-bumper duel over who had the right of way.

★ After a fatal accident on the M1 motorway north of London in 1960, the skid marks of the car were measured at 950 feet long.

★ An exploding jerry-can in a car caused the death of the driver and three passengers as well as nine passengers in the coach it collided with on a country road in France.

Suggestion box

The individual can only do so much to improve road safety. Here are a few of my suggestions to governments and manufacturers:

Softer cars. Streamlined foam padding on cars adds little to weight or wind resistance, yet can lessen countless injuries to pedestrians, cyclists and other road users.

More rights for pedestrians. The pedestrian very rarely harms the motorist. In California, the pedestrian always has right of way, even when illegally jaywalking. Other governments should adopt such laws.

Low speed limits in busy streets. In shopping streets, for instance, there could be a maximum of 15 mph at peak hours.

More manufacturer emphasis on safety and economy, less on speed.

Improved public transport systems. Less traffic means less accidents, less pollution and less waste of vital resources.

take in these orthodox points of motoring behaviour that will have the maximum impact on your safety:

Don't tailgate! Keep three car lengths away from the vehicle in front – four or five when at high speeds. Tailgating is deadly sport.

Maintain your car in perfect order. This costs money, but it's well spent. One-fifth of accidents are ascribed to defective vehicles.

Drive slowly. This point is obvious, yet overlooked. A crash at 40 miles per hour does *four* times as much damage as one at 20.

Don't drink and drive. Many people continue to risk their lives for a few pints. Well over 40 per cent of accidents have some 'alcohol content'.

Ignore the other drivers' behaviour. The best drivers control their emotions, always. Never take offence.

See and be seen. Evidence suggests that light-coloured cars, more visible in dark or dirty weather, are safer. Always turn on headlights at dusk. Accident rates go up 22 per cent in the twilight period.

Keep window, windscreens, mirrors clean. Many accidents result from restricted vision, particularly in icy conditions.

No petrol in the boot. In an accident a big blaze inside the car could kill anyone momentarily trapped.

Above all – never let your concentration stray for an instant. Think ahead too, don't just think for yourself – think on behalf of other road users, for their attention might be wandering at a fateful moment.

THE PEDESTRIAN
At the bottom of the pile

There is a growing dilemma for the walker. As an exerciser you are being encouraged more and more that you should keep striding out to get fit; yet as a user of the roads you are being employed as everybody's knock-down target. Nobody cares deeply enough about your well-being; we seem to worry far more about motorists' rights.

In Britain especially we are lagging behind the world in looking after the safety of our two-legged road users. To quote the government's own statistical publication, *Road Accidents*: 'the most worrying aspect of all is that Britain's pedestrian fatality rate compares unfavourably with some countries, notably Sweden, the Netherlands, Norway and Japan.' Even in America, the rate is well below ours.

One must blame both the government for not doing enough and the individual driver for not accepting in his heart that the pedestrian has an equal and lawful right on the roads. Ever tried crossing at a busy crossroads where there are no pedestrian lights to insist on your free passage for you? Yet even in gung-ho America any driver will patiently wait for the last of the pedestrians to saunter across before daring to move. Here is just one safety attitude that the government should be spending millions on publicizing.

After all, pedestrians are a major category of road user – the statisticians have owlishly calculated that one in three of all journeys, and 90 per cent of those shorter than a mile, are made on foot. Yes, and 2000 of them each year end in death, another 200,000 in injury.

No one is obliging the motorist forcefully enough to give

FOOTING IT FEATLY

- ★ By the end of today at least one child will have been killed on the road in Britain – and a further 120 injured.

- ★ Most child pedestrian casualties are boys.

- ★ Although children (under fifteens) are only 20 per cent of the population they suffered 39 per cent of pedestrian casualties.

- ★ In 1870 more than 1400 road deaths were recorded in Britain, all involving horses or horse-drawn traffic.

- ★ The first recorded perambulator death was in 1880.

A new law needed

Have you ever met a driver who admits an accident was his fault?

California law provides the best protection for pedestrians: motorists are *always* in the wrong. This may not appeal to the British sense of fair sport, where pedestrians are treated as targets, but it prevents casualties. If you cross a road in California, even illegally, the driver will always give way (though a policeman may book you for jaywalking). Californians know a bit about cars, so they may have hit on a good notion here.

Let's hope HMG will consider introducing legislation of this type.

priority at all times to his frail fellow road user. The motorist, except for the most spoilt of chauffeur-driven tycoons, is also a pedestrian on occasion, but once inside the car its the Mr Hyde half which emerges.

Of course motor-bikes are the most dangerous type of vehicle for street knock-downs, and even the gentle pedal cyclist kills eight or nine pedestrians a year.

One illuminating little fact: pedestrian casualties rise towards the end of the year, in November and December, the likely reason being increased shopping and drinking pre-Christmas. Out of this a great deal can be deduced. First, of course, we should watch the road-hounds more carefully than ever at that period, but secondly we have to take a share of the blame ourselves as pedestrians. Note this incriminating evidence against us: as many as 30 per cent of pedestrians killed are found to have drunk above the legal limit laid down for car drivers! Don't forget that it is an offence for a pedestrian, too, to be drunk on a highway. So don't drink and stride.

Unexplained and worrying is the case of the 10- to 14-year-olds: the rate of killed and seriously injured in this group is increasing steadily, where others are mostly dropping. There is a kind of double disaster in this, because each person dying in a young group is many times more of a loss to the community than are older people, as each has so many years still to live. The concept of 'Years of Life Lost' in a death is today being adopted as a measure of tragedy, rather than the simple total of deaths (see Way 90 and Quiz).

Teaching every pedestrian good habits, particularly the young, will have a salutary effect on preserving life as well as on YLL, Years of Life Lost. Meanwhile protective laws must be brought in to see that the motorist makes a contribution too.

ALLSPORTS
Take your pick

Many people are put off sport in their impressionable years. Memories of a gashed knee, public humiliation or three boring hours at Third Man leave their mark. Some thrive at school sportsdays, while others sneak off for a quick fag behind the bike sheds.

Sport, however, is not only essential for good health, it's a lot of fun. It's just a matter of getting into the habit: after a few weeks it becomes a pleasure. You won't just find physical exhilaration – you'll make new friends, see new places and feel happier.

You don't have to limit yourself. A quiet game of bowls on a warm summer's evening is the perfect complement to a football match in the snow. If you can afford it, don't deny yourself the joy of skiing; if your pennies are few you can still try a more exotic pastime such as hurling or high diving. Sport can reach other parts, too: many a romance has blossomed in the chilly environs of the local ice-rink. If you're unemployed or on benefits you'll find that some councils offer reduced admission to sports facilities. Take advantage of this rare generosity.

The true tale of Peter (not his real name) is a case in point. At school he was a fat, flat-footed lad, subject of much scorn and derision. In desperation he was put into a rowing boat, and, lo! he turned out to be a nifty oarsman. The happy ending came some years later at the Los Angeles Olympics: he won a gold medal for his country. So there's always hope, however bad you might think you are. You may not win a medal, but you'll win something a lot more valuable – extra years of active life.

ALL ROUNDERS

Charlotte Dod and Charles Burgess Fry were marvellously versatile athletes in the late Victorian and early Edwardian eras, before the modern specialization and professionalization of sport.

Dod won Wimbledon five times, the British Ladies Golf Championship once, an Olympic silver in archery, and played hockey for England. She was a first-class skater and tobogganist.

Fry set a world long jump record, played international soccer, first-class rugby, and captained the England cricket team. He relaxed with fishing rod and tennis racquet.

Here are a few of the less conventional sports to try your hand at:

★ Rounders and baseball. Cheap and enjoyable. All you need is a bat and ball.
★ Fencing. Excellent exercise for body and mind. Develops poise and self-confidence.
★ Handball. Good for all the limbs. Very popular in some countries.
★ Triathlon. A marathon, a two-mile swim and a 120-mile bike ride. For the very determined.
★ Pelota. A form of super squash, popular in Spain. Said to be fastest sport of all.
★ Netball and basketball. Excellent physically and socially. Growing in popularity.
★ Table tennis. Cheap and good for a rainy night. 80,000 league players.
★ Left football. Same rules as football – but you can only touch the ball with your left foot. New sport with some popularity among the sophisticates.
★ Volleyball. Excellent for health and friendship. Can be played indoors or out, with men, women and children. Most popular indoor sport in world.
★ Bicycle polo. Now recognized at international level.
★ Gymnastics. Graceful, with high fitness quotient.
★ Yachting. Expensive, but marvellous. Boats, can, of course, be rented.
★ Rugby polo. Similar to water polo, but played in a shallow pool.
★ Scuba. Can be learned in your local swimming pool. Very dangerous if no proper tuition.
★ Fijian football. Rules as football, but the game ends when both sides have the same score.
★ Australian rules football. Gets huge crowds Down Under. May well rule here too one day.
★ American football. Already popular here. Kit is expensive and laws difficult to learn. Causes many injuries, even deaths, in the USA.
★ Martial arts. Many disciplines – karate, judo, kung-fu etc. Good for fitness and, of course, self-protection.
★ Eton wall game. All you need is a ball and a wall. In the original version goals are only scored occasionally in a century.

You can always invent your own game, bearing in mind the requirements of your family and friends. Remember, fresh air and exercise are two of the key ways in which you can expand your life.

CANOEING
Winning fitness on the water

Canoeing is one of the danger sports, though it compensates for this by being well up on the list of fitness sports. The canoeist has a particular kind of fitness, perhaps not as appropriate for long life as the runner's – not solely aerobic – but with exceptional upper body fitness.

This is illustrated by the Zambesi ferrymen, those magnificent specimens, far more impressive, however, when seen sitting at the paddles than standing upright in their boats. Their physique is notable for broad shoulders, huge chests . . . and underdeveloped thighs.

The canoeist, as physiologist Craig Sharp has said, runs with his arms; the work is done entirely with the arms, displacing the water with the blades of the paddle. Not even the rower does this. The ideal of the canoeist is to pull to the blade, which is relatively fixed in the water. The technique of slicing the blade in at exactly the right angle is what counts, and the paddler needs to spend a great deal of time training in the water to perfect this technique, thus getting in plenty of physical training.

To improve aerobic status a top canoeist will spend hours a week in interval training, bursts of sustained high speed efforts, as well as developing aerobic capacity even further with running, swimming or circuit training.

If you are looking for a beautiful sport to take up you may not want to handle it so competitively, yet you will still benefit greatly from the activity. It will develop upper body strength, improve suppleness and keep down the level of body fat, making it altogether a suitable prospect for many people. Women sprint and slalom internationals are notably low on body fat.

Danger? Well, it depends how you read the statistics. Expressed academically in terms of 'deaths per million participant-hours', it is higher up the tree of risk than football, running or skiing, but in actual fact there are few serious injuries – because, of course, there are not millions of active canoeists.

A good aquatic alternative to canoeing, with fine aerobic value and stimulation of the back, limbs and brain, is windsurfing, also called sailboarding. For this you need a board, a sail and a wetsuit – all of which will set you back anything upwards of £350. There are clubs all around the country and membership costs are low.

Windsurfers like to race, at all levels, and are pressing for international recognition. Windsurfing is said to be the fastest growing sport in the world.

DICING WITH DEATH
Brinkmanship in sport

The sporting instinct is deep down a desire to dice with death. The ski-jumper enjoys that sense of brinkmanship, that 'vertigo' as she whooshes up and away. The racing driver's pride is to crash at 200 mph and climb out unhurt. The mountain climber challenges Death, 'because it is there'. The boxer and the footballer are taking part in mock battle; the body contact they enjoy is a risky reminder of the awful reality. Even small children revel in that wild roller-coaster sensation in the pit of the stomach as they're swung up in the air; they're learning to live with fear and actually like it.

That's the cardinal value of sport to the animal species: it's a training for the ultimate perils of life, a preparation, a rehearsal for horrific acts such as war. And yet taking part is perfectly enjoyable, as can be seen not only in the sportsperson or the child on a swing, but in a cub daring to nip the heels of the king of beasts.

In many another way sport contributes to a long and healthy life, in the exercising of body and mind for instance – the modern philosophers of medicine say it is dangerous *not* to exercise. Yet the anomaly of sport is that sporting persons often find themselves very close to dire danger, endangering the prospect of that long life. Racing drivers are killed, mountain climbers fall a thousand feet, boxers become punch drunk. But the aim is not to do away with sport; on the contrary, to encourage it further.

Sport aims to take the risk out of conflict; we must learn to remove the risk from sport – not to banish the excitement and thrill but to limit the dangers to life and limb with sensible precautions and reliable equipment.

The cricketer must wear a helmet, the boxer a helmet too, the footballing rules must be tightened up, the skier instructed in reducing injury, the racing driver protected and cosseted – and playgrounds must be made utterly safe, so that children can be swung high enough to feel that delicious fear at the end of the pendulum, without our fearing they will hit asphalt on the way down.

Children! Today 40 per cent of those at school smoke cigarettes. To them no doubt smoking fits perfectly the definition of sport: it is dashing, daring, and after all a great risk to life – they certainly know that well enough. It is more important than ever to let them understand that it is not a glamorous pastime, not a try-out for life. Smoking must not be thought of as sport, or associated with it.

87

AIR TRAVEL
Safe flying, happy landings

As your Inter City train speeds along at 100 mph do you stare through the window, shivering at the prospect of an ugly death?

'No way!' you'll respond, glibly quoting the latest statistics: 'Out of every billion kilometres travelled by rail only .45 of a person is killed. Safer than staying in bed. One can expect to survive 1000 lifetimes of such journeying.'

Very knowledgeable of you, and enough reason to sit back and relax. You should know that the statistics are pretty well as reassuring for flying, the second safest travel method – just 1.4 deaths per billion, i.e., a survival rate of many hundreds of lifetimes. Whereas going by car is 20 times as risky as rail, and being a motorcycle passenger 700 times. Yet do you see the car driver or pillion rider turning pale when entering a turbulent patch of road?

Surveys show though, that in spite of this logic, some 50 passengers per jumboload are scared of flying . . . they clutch their seatbelts, close their eyes, turn pale during turbulence, drown themselves in drink, wish they were back on the ground. Probably many more suffer silently, at the expense of a deal of

FLIGHTY FACTS

★ Two notable English channel crossings have been achieved in the last few years. In 1979 a pedalled aircraft got across; and in 1981 a craft powered solely by solar energy made the trip.

★ The first regular transatlantic service started in June 1939. It took nearly 19 hours from Newfoundland to Southampton, and cost £140 return.

★ It was the French who served the first hot meals on an airliner, sometime in the 1920s.

★ The largest airline is the Russian Aeroflot. In terms of passengers carried, it is more than twice as big as its nearest rival.

★ The first airline disaster on a scheduled flight happened at Golders Green, London in 1920. Four passengers jumped out at the last moment and survived. Two passengers and two crew members perished.

inner stress, which itself is extremely debilitating.

The usual reason for people's fear of flying is that they feel they have no control over the plane. If the slightest little thing goes wrong, it could start falling, and – it's so far from the ground! This is one time when your average unimaginative holidaymaker develops great fantasy power and sees engines actually coming unscrewed at their attachments, windows shattering next to him or fire curling out of the engine pod. And what of that strange sudden change of pitch in the jet noise? Could it be the first little warning, which perhaps the captain ought to know about?

Even before a flight do you wonder whether it is a safe enough airline you have booked into, whether you should have flown at night, whether you should have asked for a seat right near the front . . . OK, first-class, blow the expense! Perhaps a safer way to South America would be by coach?

Your first defence against these fancies and the stress they will be imposing on you, and frankly stress itself is the greatest peril from air travel, is to recite the hard logic of the statistics over and over while you're still in the airport lounge. Do not vex yourself about the position of your seat, or the state of the weather, or bomb risks, or the safety record of the particular aircraft . . . all are quite insignificant in the overall picture.

So that's the lesson: there is no need for any precautions at all, no more than with rail travel. The only important thing is not to worry.

Though one's own tendency to worry is the only thing to fear, that's no reason why we shouldn't keep on agitating for a still better safety record; we want the airlines to reduce statistical risks further yet, with the use of new and safer materials and with increased research into airplane design and evacuation methods. Furthermore they should be concerned to go on improving aircrew and ground staff training. Treat our guardians well! (It is noteworthy that some small increase in the US air accident rates in the early 1980s was explained as due to inexperienced workforce and staff fatigue in the wake of President Reagan's too-tough beating down of the air traffic controllers' strike in 1981 – 11,000 were sacked.)

Cheap supersonic flight is another route for the airlines to go, another suitable research project for them to plough profits into in helping to ensure a long and happy life for their passengers. Here are the logical steps in the argument: the shorter the flight the less the jeg lag; the less the lag the less the stress; and the less the stress – the more the worthwhile years of life for the passenger. That is the important consideration in air travel today, and, recognizing this, a new medical discipline is coming into existence to deal with it. It is aerophobics, the science of air travel anxiety.

88

SAFER TRAVEL
Good health on holiday

Generally speaking, you are most likely to get ill on holiday in tropical and sub-tropical countries. Yet many of the most interesting places to visit are in Asia, Africa, South America and Australasia. So you pays your fare and you takes your chances.

The hot countries are far safer these days, thanks to vaccination, drugs and improved social conditions. Not so long ago, West Africa was the 'white man's grave'; a lot of black men, women and children died there too. Much has changed, but you'd still be well advised to think about your possible risks before setting out to exotic climes. The tropics, by definition, are enormously rich in life forms, and that includes the deadly ones. The current scourge, AIDS, most likely evolved in Africa – the hot climate encourages the mutation and replication of new viruses. The dreaded *Anopheles* mosquito, carrier of malaria, has likewise mutated, and developed a new, insecticide-resistant form. But wouldn't it be wonderful to see the Taj Mahal and the wildlife of Africa, not to mention the Amazon!

Yellow fever, typhoid, cholera, hepatitis, malaria, schisto-

TSK! TSK! TSETSE

★ Tsetse flies, the carriers of sleeping sickness, hate fluorescent lights – the flicker drives them dotty. Travellers have used these lights for protection.

★ African haemorrhagic fever (Marburg-Ebola disease) is a frightful viral infection that often leads to death within a week. It was first described in Germany in 1967, where it had been acquired from green monkeys imported from Uganda.

★ Chagas disease, a common infection in Central and South America, can be transmitted by 'kissing bugs', friendly little beasts that feed on the lips and other bodily parts.

★ Snake bites reputedly kill 30–40,000 people a year. Brazil and Burma are top of this league.

★ Watch out for the blue-ringed octopus – its painless bite can kill.

★ In the USA, up to 300 people a year are killed by lightning. Rather more in Zimbabwe.

Safeways

If you're travelling to a country that harbours exotic diseases, make sure you get all your shots *early*. It can often take time for an immunization to become effective. This applies especially to business travellers, who may have to set off at a moment's notice.

If bitten by a snake, you should obviously get to a hospital as soon as possible. Try and kill the snake (taking care *not* to get bitten again) and take its corpse with you. This will enable the hospital staff to identify it and apply the appropriate treatment.

somiasis (bilharzia), rabies, lassa fever, yaws, AIDS and plague – just to mention a few of the delights that await you. Most of them are preventable or avoidable, though. They thrive in different countries, so your first step should be to find out from your doctor which of them abound at your intended destination. Most vaccinations are not compulsory (though that for yellow fever is), but many are available. As the doctor said, the best preventive measure, except for malaria, is *common sense*.

In endemic areas, malaria is more dangerous than all other infections put together. Apart from protecting yourself with insect repellents and insecticide spray in your room or bed nets, you would be wise to take recommended anti-malarial tablets from the moment you enter a malarious country, and for thirty days after you leave it. If you feel unwell on your return, see your doctor, and ask to be referred to a specialist.

Make sure food is cooked properly – this will kill worms and parasites. There are treatments for parasites (often called 'helminths'), but you'd be better off not acquiring any in the first place. Fresh water is often dangerous, so it's better not to swim, or even paddle in it – bilharzia nips in quickly.

Medical insurance won't cost much, and will certainly ease your mind. A nice, neat first-aid kit will not occupy much space in your baggage. Treat yourself.

If you've already had a serious illness, such as a coronary, you should take special care to research your journey thoroughly. Flying can be tricky if you're not properly recovered, and a hot, humid climate can strain the old ticker. Severe anaemia, recent stroke and severe sinusitis, among other conditions, make flying inadvisable. There are always trains, boats and motor vehicles.

Don't worry too much, though. An enormous number of people travel all over the world, and most suffer nothing more serious than diarrhoea. Worry itself can make you ill.

Watch out for tigers.

STREET PROOFING
The new noble art of self-defence

The martial arts prove a little daunting for those looking for personal safety in the streets, especially for women, who lack size and fighting form anyway and might not be kitted out in just the right baggy judo gear at the moment the mugger strikes. As a result other streetwise disciplines, thought to be more practical, are now coming up instead.

It seems that many women are fearful of walking out after dark, so they do need help – and let it be practical. According to a London survey 40 per cent are in this category. It is sad if true that they should be so over-anxious, for in fact the statistical chances of being bag-snatched, let alone raped, are minimal. It's the Press, which does not like to hurry over the salacious details of a rape or murder incident, that has made it seem today as if violence is reaching out everywhere and going on all the time. Yet among our 50,000,000 population the number of serious cases is in fact tiny.

Ask yourself how many people you have ever known who have been involved. Nor has the incidence increased in historic terms; the reverse – no working-class woman was safe for long in the grim, Victorian inner-city streets.

So it's advisable to keep fear in proportion. But that's no reason not to get trained in counter-attack; the training itself can be rewarding, while the fitness gained, and the confidence that comes out of being strong and fit, will help many a woman, and many a man, in their daily lives.

One of the new techniques, Streetproofing, designed by ex-martial arts teachers, includes safety procedures as well as fighting instruction. Frankly, it's hard to see how a woman (or for that matter a man), even if well-trained, can put one over on a large lout who has the additional advantage of surprise on his side, so it's wise of this movement to put a lot of weight into showing people how to anticipate and avoid dangerous situations; and how to identify a threat swiftly so that at the least they can be off in a flash, or act very fierce, serving to put off an assailant.

One of the Streetproofing principles is to teach women to expect brutality and thus to react ferociously themselves – steeled to inflict injury. Kicks and blows, viciously aimed, are what's recommended, rather than a mere slap in the face, especially if you suspect a desperate attack.

Then finally there is emphasis on 'after-service' techniques: reporting to the police and exercising legal rights.

This kind of training might become more widely popular with

Neighbourhood watch

If you don't take a training course in street defence, you should at least be extra careful in the way you move around the seedier highways. Here are a few hints from Alix Kirsta's *Book of Stress Survival*.

★ Don't walk alone after dark through deserted ill-lit streets, even as a short-cut.

★ Walk confidently and briskly.

★ If you see someone suspicious approach, go to the front door of the nearest occupied building and ring the bell, as if you're expected.

★ Never wait alone at a bus stop.

★ No lifts from strangers.

★ Beware of multi-storey car parks.

★ Do not open your front door to anyone whose identity you are not sure of.

★ Walk on the kerb side of the pavement to avoid being grabbed by someone in a doorway.

And I might add: keep your high-heeled shoes in the cupboard.

women, who were not always comfortable with the rather competitive and sporting side of the martial activities. They were concerned enough to join a course but most would drop out at the very beginning.

It's society's duty to make the street environment safer for women, and to do it so resolutely that women are prevailed into *feeling* that they are safe. This requires in the long run a better adjusted community but the immediate need is for extra policing and for the police rank and file to show solicitude for any woman attacked.

In fact in the last year or two the police handling of rape complainants *has* begun to improve – the officer no longer starts with the idea that the offence has somehow been invited by the woman herself. This has led to an increase in the number of women willing to come forward and make reports, to an increase in the number of cases entered on the files, and finally to increased public awareness of street violence – and thus, paradoxically, to increased nervousness in the ranks of women.

SPORTING FATALITIES
Higher rise, higher risk

The most dangerous sports are those that take place above ground level – the higher you are the harder you fall. Some are aerial sports, such as hang gliding and parachute jumping, while others depend on extreme downhill speed such as skiing.

You take the chance of underestimating the riskiness of these sports if you look merely at the absolute number of participants killed – perhaps no more than 50 per year in this country, out of a death roll from all causes of more than half a million. No, the point is that when you consider how few people go in for the altitude sports, the number of fatalities per million actual participants per year is quite substantial. That's the scientific way of measuring the risk, and the fair way.

The Royal Society's Study Group has come up with figures on accidental death rates in sport that show sport-parachuting as having by far the highest rate of deaths for every million participants during a year – 1900. One might believe that caving was a pretty dangerous game, but that scores only 45 in comparison.

In another set of figures, rock climbing was shown as some four times more dangerous than canoeing – and 80 times more than boxing! (British figures for skiing are not so easily analysed because of course most British ski casualties occur in Europe,

---

TALL STORIES

★ Eiger means 'ogre'. This wicked mountain has claimed the lives of at least 40 of the world's finest climbers. Sherpa Tenzing, conqueror of Everest, tried it once, but turned back, saying: 'Too difficult! Too dangerous!'

★ An American climber, John Gill, was able to do six one-arm pull-ups in a row using either hand. He could also do one-finger pull-ups with the index or middle finger.

★ Some American hang gliders have made 'thermal' flights of 100 miles. Thermals are uprushes of warm air, favoured by swifts and other birds.

★ Ski flying differs from ski jumping, in that the emphasis is purely on distance, with little regard to style. The 500 ft barrier has been beaten.

★ Gliders have managed speeds of 100 mph, distances of 1000 miles in a day, and altitudes of 46,000 ft.

Your way to the top

★ *Always* obey rules. As Nigel Mansell, a keen amateur helicopterist, says: 'I do this by the book. If you make a mistake in this game, you can really get hurt.'

★ Fitness is of great importance. Running, weight-work and other strenuous exercise will prepare you and lessen your chances of a fatal accident.

★ Study and learn. Magazines and books will be on offer at your local library. Take advantage of this free service.

★ Phone contacts: British Parachute Association: 0533–597788; British Association of Parascending Clubs: 01–439 2465; British Gliding Association: 0533–51051; British Hang Gliding School: 0959–73996; British Ski Federation: 01–235 8227.

not documented in home statistics. This last winter there was a high number of ski and mountain tragedies in Europe – in Scotland, too, the mountain climbing toll was high.)

In spite of these death rates it is unlikely that anyone is going to want to campaign against people taking part in exciting sports (though they do against boxing in spite of its lower risk rate). These activities bring real benefits to the individuals – in other words they are great fun – and all the world admires the nerve of the athletes concerned.

Still, there are lessons to apply, sport by sport, in providing effective back-up, so that we can limit the dangers. This might mean safer equipment, as in hang gliding; better body protection, as in skiing; or better rescue procedures, as in climbing. Each sport needs to look to its own needs.

There's an additional way of observing the problem, using another scientific measuring rule: how many years of prospective active life is lost per casualty? Obviously most of these deaths happen to people in their twenties and thirties, who have scores of years of valuable life left. They will not only be mourned deeply by their families, maybe leaving young children, but their loss is sure to be felt especially severely by the whole community . . . they have more yet to give than an elderly invalid, say.

Science calibrates this in terms of Years of Life Lost, YLL. Thus a mountain climber aged 30 lost in an avalanche has maybe robbed us of 50 years of his life, whereas the invalid of 75 has only five or ten years left on average; i.e. the climber loss is up to ten times as serious a matter for the community.

WAYS

91~99

SERENDIPITY

Modern society can blind us to the wondrous diversity of nature. Because so many of us inhabit the same kinds of cities, and watch the same kinds of TV programmes, it can be easy to forget just how rich and varied life can be. And yet, to keep ourselves fit and healthy, bright and happy, we *need* change, we need colour, we need to make full use of all the multifarious possibilities that can be squeezed into a brief 100 years.

In this final section are another nine ways in which you might be able to inspire yourself to live longer. On the one hand I recommend indulgence, for what is life without the pleasure of a new pair of sheets or a quite unnecessary trip to the theatre? On the other hand and contrariwise, much research shows that exposing yourself to hunger and cold can do wonders for the constitution. Think back a few hundred years to a time when we were closer to nature: no central heating in the winter and not much work in the summer; frugality in February and stuffing yourself in September.

Feeling tense? Fraught? On edge? Instead of relying on valium, why not try massage? If you can't afford a professional masseur, learn to do it yourself. It's easy to learn and can do wonders for those stiffnesses in the neck and shoulders. You can do it to music, too. Massage and Mozart – a little corner of paradise.

Diversity is the key. Nature herself is wondrously diverse, so let's take a lead from Her. God thought it fit to create the hippopotamus, so why should we feel self-conscious about playing the tuba? Or even inventing a new instrument? Stop talking and start playing something . . . for a few pounds you can avail yourself of a guitar and serenade your friends into the early hours.

And finally, a humble presentation of six small Christmas gifts. Look at the 99th Way well before 25 December; the date, as it happens, of the author's birthday, exactly two-thirds of a century ago.

S.R.S.
August 1987

91

FRIENDSHIP
Eh amigo!

'. . . the fire of soul is kindled at the taper of conwiviality, and the wing of friendship never moults a feather!'

Charles Dickens

In the past much of our emotional and material support came from the family. Not just mum and dad, brothers, sisters and children, but from the whole extended range of Rabbit's relations. In many small tribes people are aware in precise detail of the exact nature of their relationships. They can enumerate third cousins twice-removed and other obscure beings.

However, in our modern industrial society all has changed. For a start, families tend to be smaller. Even in China the one-child family is now the norm. Secondly, members of families often live far apart – Jack is in Australia, Mabel in Canada and Zeke is cruising about in South America. Divorce is more common, and single parents are everywhere. All this may or may not be a good thing, but it certainly is the case, and it's most likely going to carry on that way.

Which brings us to the matter of friendship. More and more it looks as though people will find help and support in times of need (not to mention fun and laughter) among their friends. Friends at work, friends at play; friends around the corner and friends across the globe; friends in the football team and in the string quartet.

Making new friends can sometimes be difficult, especially if you're a bit shy. Even children, when they first meet, will blush or turn aside. But usually they're as cheerful as cheese after a few minutes. For grown-ups, the acquired defences of a lifetime may need more breaking down. It has been noted that women find friendships more easily than men – perhaps because they are not so frightened to show their feelings, and not so intent on competition and self-assertion. Men take note! The ladies regularly outlive you by six or seven years.

There are many advantages to friendship. You can choose your friends whereas you can't choose your relatives. You can cross all kinds of racial, national and cultural boundaries on the wing of friendship, enriching your knowledge and experience. Who knows, before you look twice, you might have lost a friend and gained a lover – or vice versa. For many people, a life of close and caring friendship is the only way to survive.

Just to take it one step further: if the consideration and tolerance we associate with friendship could be extended from nation to nation, we might all get the chance to live 100 years.

HUMOUR
Laugh until it stops hurting

A good laugh is clearly the best medicine to be had, it's quite a shame they don't do a tickling machine on the national health. Laughter may not be able to help a great deal with your ingrowing toenails or outbreaks of wind, but it's a marvel when it comes to that old devil Stress, really among the most serious of the conditions besetting us all.

There can be nothing so effective in releasing tension as a good guffaw, or one of those rollicking waves of guffaws that seize you and go on and on until you're quite helpless, worried even that your heart won't survive the onslaught. You can positively feel the poisons dissolving away as the body is taken by its very scruff and given a sound shaking.

Humour secondly assists in putting things in their proper place, it cuts down the pompous and earnest upstarts among your thoughts. It gives you to realize that you may have been exaggerating the seriousness of your worries about life's depressing little problems of the moment. We only have to recall the case of that famous psychiatric patient who complained of the frightful stress he was exposed to at work.

'Ah, I see,' responded his doctor ponderously. 'Ah, stress. But excuse me, not perhaps stress; your job is grading eggs, not so?'

'That's it, doc,' wailed the patient. 'All the time, decisions,

---

THE VERY BEST OF MEDICINE

★ Humour therapy is now a form of treatment in American hospitals.

★ Laughter calms human arousal mechanisms, reduces the output of adrenal glands. This brings down stress.

★ A Frenchwoman, Julie Hette, hires herself out as a professional laugher, at 300 francs an hour. She comes with a guarantee to make you laugh.

★ In New Guinea, among the Fore tribesmen, the exotic disease kuru was, until recently, the most common cause of death. Symptoms included hysterical laughter for little apparent reason. It was discovered that the agent responsible for the illness was transmitted by the eating of human brains, a practice done as a mark of respect for the dead. Since the cause was eradicated, the incidence of the disease has declined rapidly.

Smile please

Now what are you to do if you can't see the humorous side to things? Nothing ever makes you burst out laughing, not even your own jests? Is there some course you can take? Any organization to join?

Here's a test to check if you have any potential. Read the above joke about the eggsorter once again, to see if it can make you laugh.

Didn't work? Try once more, then if things remain hopeless, your best solution is to apply to the French Foreign Legion. They're still accepting recruits; you can say you're joining up in order to forget a bad joke.

In any case, don't worry!

decisions! Grade 1, Grade 2? – Grade 2, Grade 1? Decisions the whole day.'

A sense of humour might have brought his tension down a peg or two, at the expense of an occasional misfit in the eggworld.

Of course you can't so easily go out and get hold of a sense of humour if you entirely lack one. But you can do something: you can seek out the company of the good-natured and good-humoured. Some of it will rub off on you, for certain. Or get yourself a jester – the role was invented for defeating depression. Even kings, in spite of their top positions, needed to be got over their disappointments from time to time and they could afford to employ jesters to help them see things in perspective. The recipe the jesters used was to cut them down to size. It could be tricky, so they needed to dress it up in jocular form.

Of course the jester himself, not being a king, had early on learned to make the best of his lowly position by poking fun at himself, thus acting as his own jester. When he duly became expert at putting things in an amusing, cheeky and cynical light, he was promoted to a job at court, where he could get away with impudent put-downs aimed at his bosses and betters.

You may need to find your own jester in fiction or film. Keep imbibing a good diet of the stuff. On celluloid there is to be recommended the Marx Brothers, to name but a few, or one of those dear old BBC comedy series.

The main thing is to laugh. And when you feel a good laugh coming on, don't restrain it, don't be too British, be sure to let go. Abandon your inhibitions; sit back and bray away at your loudest . . . until the tears pour out.

You might then switch over to tragedy and allow those tears to flow. Quite as beneficial as a laugh in dealing with tension, after all, is a good old cry.

177

MUSIC
Food of life and love

Music hath healing powers. Here is a good example:

Anita had spent much of her life in psychiatric hospitals. Her two marriages ended tragically, and her children spent time in orphanages while she underwent the full range of treatment: LSD, ECT, therapy and drugs. At 55 her life seemed over . . . but it was not to be. One of the helpful elements in the creation of her new life (and now she's thriving as she approaches 70) was the choir. The joy of music, the pleasure of new friends, and the pleasure of *giving* pleasure to others through singing: perhaps it was these that tipped the balance back over towards sanity.

Generally speaking musicians turn out to be a long-lived band. Segovia is strumming well into his 90s; Casals reached 96; Rubinstein 94; Sibelius 91; Boult 93; Stokowski 95; Tertis 98; and, of course, Eubie Blake made it to 100 before he played the final bar. Younger types include Stravinsky, 88; Toscanini, 89; and Bliss, 83.

Why is it that music might extend your life? Perhaps it's because it keeps your feet on the ground (you have to practise)

MUSICAL NOTES

★ Constantijn Huygens reached the age of 90 in the seventeenth century. Apart from his distinguished musical career, he was an outstanding poet, dramatist and politician. He regularly dabbled in art, science and gymnastics.

★ Hildegard of Bingen was one of the best composers of the Middle Ages. In her long life she also won fame as a writer, mystic and diplomat.

★ Jazz and rock drummers are often particularly fitness-conscious – and they need to be. Their favourite sports include competitive walking, running, swimming, tennis and volleyball.

★ Whistles and flutes from 20,000 years ago have been found in Russia and Hungary.

★ Two of the compositions of Johann Strauss include parts for a rifle.

Start up a song

There are two reasons why people can't (or won't) play music. The first is technical – it takes effort to practise and study.

The second, and perhaps the more significant, is psychological – people are too shy or self-conscious to try, even though they may love music passionately. For this I suggest: find a comfortable level. There is a theory that says composers are failed performers and conductors are failed instrumentalists. Just think! Beethoven found his own level.

Try it in company – join a choir. Don't forget the Portsmouth Sinfonia, an orchestra only open to people who can't play.

and at the same time gives you a glimpse of Heaven. Music is the oldest and most natural of the arts – even birds and whales sing – so maybe it keeps one in touch with the reality of the natural life. The taste of beauty feeds the appetite for life. Contrariwise the physical effort of blowing a trumpet or conducting an orchestra makes for good exercise.

It doesn't matter what you do, or where you do it, but there are one or two things that will help you maximize your pleasure:

★ Try to practise three or four hours a week. It's better to do half an hour a day rather than three hours on Sunday.

★ Get together with other people. Music is always a social art, and you can usually find others around your level. Music cuts across barriers of class, age, race and sex better than anything.

★ Buy as good an instrument as you can afford. A good penny whistle (and it's a fine instrument) costs a couple of quid. A Steinway grand costs about the same as a new Jaguar.

★ Start slowly and take your time. After all, if you're going to reach 100, you'll have years before you need trouble yourself with the late Beethoven sonatas. Beatles tunes, folk songs and pop songs are a good introduction. Then you can move on to more sophisticated songwriters like Gershwin, Cole Porter and Jerome Kern. Jazz and classical tend to be the most technical and demanding, but remember that simplicity can be the most difficult thing of all.

★ Learn . . . and then teach! Teaching and learning continue throughout a musician's life. The infinite subtleties of rhythm and harmony demand attention and reconsideration.

★ Have a party. Enjoyable musical experiences can be had at home; all you need is an old guitar, a bottle of wine and a few friends.

★ SING.

94

SPOIL YOURSELF, GO ON!
A little of what you fancy is usually safe, often essential

Self-indulgence can be the nicest way of keeping life going merrily on and on – if not taken to the point of over-indulgence! Many of the things people believe to be inimical to fitness, just because they *like* them, are in fact not only harmless taken in moderation but positively necessary for complete good health. Alcohol for one, luscious foodstuffs, sex, anger, tears, even pure and contented laziness. The very pleasures and purposes of life, and some would banish them!

Ask any runner how the ignorant giggle wickedly when offering alcohol, assuming an athlete would never touch the stuff, whereas runners are famous sozzlers, though rarely getting paralytic and able to go for days without missing their snort; certainly not alcoholics.

The ignorant get their lead from the modern keep-alive movement, many of whose philosophers and priests are prudish – poor things, harshly brought up, one supposes. They broadcast the idea that anything just that little bit shockingly

---

SOME GREAT OVER-INDULGERS

Over-indulgence can do you good, if it's only to get you into literature. Here is a list of some who got away with it, or almost:

Food: Sir John Falstaff, Pantagruel, Billy Bunter, Humpty Dumpty . . . and that whole cast of dozens at Gervaise's birthday party in Zola's *L'Assomoir*.

Drink: Sir John Falstaff, Colonel Chinstrap, Bacchus, Heathcliff, Sir Toby Belch.

Sleep: Sir John Falstaff, Oblomov, The Dormouse, The Fat Boy, Rip Van Winkle.

Sex: Sir J. Falstaff, Don Juan, Tom Jones, Casanova, Humbert Humbert, Nana and Mae West (or was she a real person?).

Money: Sir John F., Mr Micawber, Mammon, Scrooge, Midas, Croesus, Becky Sharp.

Practical Jokes: Sir J.F., Till Eulenspiegel.

Procrastination: S.J.F., Scarlett O'Hara, Lucky Jim, Andrew Aguecheek.

Then there are such people as in the Confessions of an Opium Eater, but we don't want to give *them* the opportunity of too much publicity . . .

Ways and means

You'll need a special budget set aside for your indulgences; the money mustn't come out of the mortgage money, or the holiday fund (or the kiddie's piggy-bank). Put it away securely for the big moment when you want to break out, but not too securely that it takes a week to get out.

Standby suggestion: if nothing's coming right, have a stack of cheap plates ready in the garden shed, which you can take out and throw ceremonially against a brick wall one by one to help you vent your spleen! (Throw them all together in one great pile, for maximum effect on spleen.)

scrumptious is to be avoided. Whereas the very opposite is usually true. A delicious feeling is the body's way of telling you that something is good for you. It *wants* what it *needs*.

Even alcohol! The fact, which astonished Science when discovering it not so long ago, is that those who enjoy a drink or two now and again not only live longer than heavy drinkers, but they actually live longer than complete teetotallers. Be prudent, not prudish. Dr Anstie long ago invented Anstie's Limit: one and a half tots a day for good health.

Now salt. You'll need to make your own judgement here, as there are no firm facts, just a great controversy among scientists as to whether too much salt does any harm. No medical researcher has been able to measure it to the satisfaction of others. The only firm evidence is for those who have high blood pressure: they can relieve it a little by a salt-free diet – though not nearly as much as by taking up mild, regular exercise.

Some branches of the medical world have gone rather far with other food fads too and have inhibited people completely against our delicious British diet. My advice: don't cut out all fats, red meat, white bread, butter, not completely.

'Dost thou think, because thou art virtuous, there shall be no more cakes and ale?' Sugar particularly deserves a word in its favour. Except for its effect on tooth decay and on potential diabetics there is only controversial evidence against it.

All you need do is keep your eating balanced – fruit and salads, nuts and fish, as well as the tasty things that have an undeserved bad reputation. The only indulgence you cannot afford, not even one puff, because of its addictiveness: smoking.

Apart from that treat yourself to a late lie-in now and again, an extra holiday, a pair of hand-made shoes, a little flutter, a little ogle. Yes, an interest in sex is one of the essentials in keeping the mind and the body toned up through a long life.

FISHING
Anglers do it sitting down

It may not be the most active of sports, fishing, but it attracts Saturday afternoon support far vaster than football's, and on that account has to be given serious thought. The question to be raised is this: does the fisherman get fair value in the matter of health and vigour?

You can't help replying disapprovingly, first of all, that a good deal of the work of angling seems to be conducted by the rod, with the owner quite passive. You even ask pointedly, is it the owner propping up the rod, or the rod the owner? Yes, is that aerobics, is that action? But steady on, you think again . . . maybe it's in this fact that can be found the very contribution angling makes to health: long sessions of compulsory de-stressing! True leisure!

Good point. And we must agree also that the fisherman does usually face a good tramp on his two legs along to his special spot and imbibes freely of oxygen all through his outing.

What more can we do for these angling millions? Encourage them to speed up the walk along to the fens or the seaside and to look to their posture at . . . no slumping on their canvas seats.

It would certainly be to their additional advantage to jump into a dinghy and row briskly to and fro before settling at their favourite hole; and if nothing else suits, why not a positive session of exercises? Double-leg jumping and arm-swinging, for no less than 12 minutes. This would not only add to their fitness, but would warm the body, ease their stiffness, pass the time and very likely serve to attract the fish.

IN AND OUT OF WATER

★ Fishing is a sport with a low mortality rate. However, anglers have been known to die when wearing waders. They step into deep water and are upended. The waders fill with air and the victims drown with their feet pointing skywards.

★ Chrysoidine dye, used to colour maggots, has lost popularity with anglers. Cases of bladder cancer have been attributed to the dye.

★ Sharks prefer to attack humans in warmer waters, close inshore. They favour the lower limbs, buttocks, forearms and hands. Mortality can be as high as 70 per cent though this would be less if first aid were available.

HUNGER & COLD
Ways to well-being?

These two states may seem like peculiar promoters of health – and of course, I'm certainly not saying that we'd all be better off cold and hungry, or that those who are through no choice of their own have got one over on us – but there is scientific and common sense evidence for the resultant long-term benefits (despite the temporary discomfort). *Don't* overdo it, though – hypothermia and anorexia can be highly dangerous.

Carefully controlled experiments on rats, fish and other animals have shown that fasting and lowering of body temperature extend lifespan. As yet no adequate explanation exists for these phenomena, though it has been suggested that the slowing down of the rate of metabolism is a major factor. In the hibernating species, such as bears or badgers, the states co-exist – food intake is minimal and body temperature drops. After all, they've probably inhabited the colder regions of the world longer than us. We only left Africa a couple of million years ago.

Fasting has a lengthy history. Many religions recommend it as essential for mental and physical well-being. Strict Muslims observe the month-long festival of Ramadan each year: food is forbidden before sunset. Jews are more economical with their fast – for just one day a year, Yom Kippur, an observant Jew must take no food. Christians give up some luxury, often a food, for Lent. Buddhists and Hindus may fast frequently.

Many non-religious people fast, perhaps missing a day a week. It is true that many modern health problems are linked to overeating, and a day a week will probably do you good. Try it for yourself. But make sure you eat properly on the other six days. Girls and young women beware – excessive fasting can lead to anorexia nervosa, a dismal and sometimes fatal disease. (You men, watch out as well. Anorexia is by no means exclusively female.)

Cold is sought by many. The very rich head for St Moritz for an invigorating few weeks on the slopes. They also retire to Swiss sanatoria to recover from their lowland excesses. The rest of us must make do with bracing winter walks, cold showers, saunas and open bedroom windows. Don't fight the cold – let it flow through your whole body, but not for too long. A chilly stroll makes a good cup of coffee even better, and it improves the appetite.

And in a hard winter, insulate your house properly for cheaper fuel bills!

97

MASSAGE
Defence against injury

Massage can be a major adjunct to sport and the healthy life. Its prime role is in defence, as a bastion *against* injury; however, when injured an athlete will make the masseur the first stop after on-the-spot work with ice on the affected muscle.

In injury prevention the aim is to keep the muscles nicely toned up and stretched out, with the blood in them circulating freely. The physiotherapist will also be checking in advance for symptoms of overuse, noting such early warning signals as stiffness, tightness or lumpiness in the muscles.

In fact the physio's job is as much diagnostic as curative. The signs being rarely visible on the surface, it is necessary to feel deep into the muscle tissue, searching out areas of tenderness, dryness or heat (heat is a sign of inflammation), as well as the more obvious lumps, bumps or knots.

Massage – osteopaths, chiropracters, remedial masseurs as well as conventional physiotherapists make use of the art – has as its objective the normalizing of the tissues.

It is the rubbing firmly along the muscle, in the direction of the heart, i.e. the direction of the blood's natural flow, that regenerates the muscle tissue through improving the blood supply to it. This calls for deep pressure on the large muscle groups, not merely a rubbing of the skin.

The effect of the massage is to hasten the re-processing work being done by the body itself when an athlete is recovering from training and competitive sessions. Muscles rendered uniformly strong are less likely to suffer out-of-balance tears. Also over-

---

THERE'S THE RUB

★ Your total body skin area covers about 17 sq ft – the skin weighs 6 lb.

★ A Japanese wrestler's body skin area measures 40 sq ft, providing the masseur with more than twice the work on an average client.

★ The word massage means literally 'to knead'.

★ As an alternative to massage, scrubbing the body with a brush will make it shine and feel good.

★ Yet another alternative is to direct strong jets of water onto the muscles.

Massage for the skin

Skin is a highly efficient organ with many jobs to do: it has to protect the body from bacteria; to eliminate waste matter; to regulate temperature; to breathe – and to serve as an attractive wrapping.

So it pays to keep it in condition.

When it's healthy, the skin is smooth and supple and has no blemishes; it glows like finest satin. But it needs help to stay healthy: just as animals spend a great deal of time on their surface coverings, so should human beings. Stroking, kneading, pinching, wringing, pressing, cupping and pummelling the skin is the way humans handle this – this is skin massage, whether carried out by expert masseurs or by Doing It Yourself. The body shows it approves of the treatment by sending back signals of enjoyment that say 'What a tonic!'

contracted muscles, their blood supply tightly throttled, are eased out.

The massage, plus stretching and the right exercise, will bring great benefit to the muscles. Flexible and full, they will not only carry the limbs more speedily through their required range of movement, but will be less likely to tear or pull when called on to make an explosive effort.

Today's top runners, both short-distance athletes and marathoners, resort more and more frequently to regular massage, as the intensity of competitive pressure increases. In other sports, too, massage is becoming more highly valued.

As an ordinary sportsman or sportswoman, having to budget your expenditure of both time and money, if lucky you will find a hospital out-patients where a sympathetic physiotherapy department might give you regular, all-year-round attention, but if not the occasional call on a professional can be supplemented by DIY treatment. You can't hope for a comprehensive diagnosis this way, nor will you be able to reach all parts as easily as another person can, but you should be able to take care of the calves and hamstrings where many problems arise.

The fundamental principle: always massage towards the heart, this helps dislodge scar tissue, to send it sailing away in the bloodstream; and use fairly slow, deep pressure. A lubricant like baby oil will make the rubbing easier. Don't work over muscle tears or varicose veins. Always see to stretching.

There are no dangers with massage, but plenty of bonuses. It guards against damage, helps healing, improves suppleness, aids relaxation – then, on top of everything, it is positively sybaritic, a treat for the body.

BEST OF FRIENDS
Dogs and cats, pals for life

One of the best aids to longevity, statistics tell us, is the possessing of a household pet. Now it's been said that statistics often lie, but it surely wouldn't come up with biased stories about animals. And anyway we've all seen that this does work out in practice, we've all known an old dame virtually kept alive by dear tabby – or kept alive by having to attend to its needs, which is much the same thing.

Many lone people of all ages, and lonesome couples, are supported by the household dog or cat, which is quite happy to provide love and understanding in return for more of the same.

All year round a pet is company, something everyone needs, an essential form of social relationship helping to reduce stress and blood pressure, both well-known enemies of long life.

Even a budgie or a bowl of fish has a good bit of company to offer . . . whereas a hamster is an absolute cageful of fun and mischief in itself, with that showoff side to its nature. There are even individuals who get on well enough with terrapins and snakes. These days, when certain people are said to be able to talk to plants, you might go so far as to make do with an indoor garden – but it doesn't seem quite the same thing really, not altogether so cuddly.

In the end the dog or cat is what the sensible old codger will go for. You can make something of their language after a little study, so there is a sort of two-way dialogue, which you don't get with the guppy or the aspidistra; they are very easy, too, when it

---

PET LIKES

★ One in ten people prefer pets to partners. One in five prefer pets to children. One in three prefer pets to their job. Nearly half claim to prefer pets to money.

★ Grief for a departed doggie can be profound. One authority recommends that vets should be given training to help them cope with the problems facing bereaved owners.

★ In California a minister has devised a religious mourning service for deceased pets.

★ A pet rabbit is on record as having survived for 18 years. Mice and hamsters will live for five years or more if properly fed and exercised.

Mutual responsibilities

Pets are not toys. They need care and attention and if they can't be taught social responsibility it's your duty to fill in for them. In some American towns you are by law obliged to clear up doggie's doings – why should the rest of us be abused, nosewise? No sir, nohow!

So kerb your dog – and *curb* your dog, do not allow attacks on passing joggers, postmen and cyclists.

Give the animal plenty of love and exercise, but not too much food. Many a beloved pet has passed away before its time due to overweight.

comes to being bossed around and luckily seem to have quite similar tastes in television programmes as their owners. Their only obstinacies are to do with the occupation of the most comfortable armchair and, especially in the case of the dog, with demands for exercise.

Ah, now this is just where the dog wins out as being the most worthwhile pet there is. For when the dog gets exercise we all get exercise! And exercise is as important an element in regard to long life as is stress . . . regular exercise right into your seventies and eighties. So you provide yourself with the best coach in the world, a dog who says come out for your outing, I need mine, and now, now, now! – bow-wow! Then you'll have to walk at least a mile; better still, put on some soft shoes and make it a run.

What dog? A labrador is a typical ideal all-rounder – calm, intelligent, but in need of plenty of exercise. Little dogs are generally over-active and can be irritating yappers, though that does at least qualify them for the post of head of security. But there are literally hundreds to choose from – one is bound to suit your likes and lifestyle.

What cat? Not so necessary to discriminate here, for the cat species is less differentiated than the dog. The Siamese is among the more fidgety and temperamental – but then they've got looks, and personality!

A warning to those who get too reliant on a pet to keep them going: how will you manage when your old friend, to put it politely, snuffs it? They don't last more than a dozen years or so, after all. The answer is soon arrived at: invest in a second animal while the old 'un is still comparatively hale, and run the two of them together. That's better than an insurance policy. There's a further advantage in that the new one will learn good manners from the old, will be taught how to accommodate to your ways and will be there to join you in a sad tear when your mutual friend finally slips away.

SCROOGE'S REVENGE
. . . or Xmas day's perilous ways

It was Scrooge's annual blow-out. Everyone was there, in-ebriated out of their little minds. 'Drink up, very good for you,' Scrooge bustled around encouraging them, 'and then try one of these fat Havanas. One for you, Wally?'

The party was noisily under way on a hired houseboat on the River Styx. Sir Walter Raleigh was one of the distinguished Souls present. He looked at Scrooge quizzically. 'Thank you, unusually generous of you,' he remarked.

'Ahah, I'm in the tobacco trade,' replied his host, with an evil grin, 'as you were once; and you know our old saying: de foist one is free. Xmas is that special occasion – tempt 'em once, then they're hooked, man.'

Elvis Presley yodelled his support from the band platform. 'Yeeehoo! And send around more of the coke, the snow, the rocks, the grass and the ice. Keep it coming, baby.'

Enjoying the feasting and fun like anything was Sir John Falstaff. He waved a chicken bone at Elvis. 'My kingdom for a capon,' he misquoted. 'Go on, Elvis, play us "Temptation"!'

Florence Nightingale took umbrage at all this. Picking up a large banner, flanked by several vestal virgins dressed in white and singing anti-smoking hymns, she advanced on Scrooge.

'Curses,' he said, reading the slogan on her banner – Save Our Souls This Xmas. He looked around for Al Capone and yelled at him: 'Get these dames outa here, whaddam I paying you protection for, Scarface?'

'Would you be wishing to have them . . . comprehensively removed, if not to say dismantled, my dear fellow?' answered Capone, who'd been taught to speak proper by Dickens himself since arriving in No Man's Land.

Florence was calling for help now, as Capone's gunmen started manhandling her. 'Stay!' she exhorted the gunmen, Scrooge, Dickens and all the guests. 'You are doing nothing but killing yourselves, not me; just as much as if you'd asked Scarface Capone to machine-gun you full of lead. Christmas is the time to give up smoking, not be turned on.'

There was jeering and booing from the trade.

'Drugs, too,' she cried heroically.

Falstaff raised a tankard of sack with an encouraging hiccup. 'Down with drugs.'

Florence turned on him. 'Down with obesity,' she retorted, 'for while there may be good fibre in Christmas pud, plenty of vitamin content in red currant jelly, and protein in turkey – too much is too much. And down with lethargy . . . instead of sleeping it off after dinner, far better would be a mile walk.'

'Down with lechery,' sobbed old Sir John, 'no, no!'

Scrooge tried some of his soft-soaping on Miss Nightingale. 'Let Sir John enjoy himself. Christmas is a time of goodwill to all men – no matter we lose one or two of them in the cause.'

When Florence started up her usual holiday sermon against over-indulgence in alcohol the crowd, led by Dylan Thomas, motherless as ever, bellowed out, 'Boring!' and began shoving her around aggressively.

Was there no gentleman would come to her aid? Yes, there was one to respond, James Dean the film actor, a true Southern gentleman. 'Quick,' he whispered, 'this way, miladyship, make for my auto.'

As they passed through the crowd she distributed leaflets calling for extra vigilance in the festive season, before gratefully allowing James Dean to whisk her off to safety.

Some wit in the crowd shouted after: 'None of your speeding, James. Not so safe to drink and drive at Christmas, with your record.'

The actor poked his head back out belligerently: 'You think I'm chicken?' he challenged.

'Remember what happened before,' cried the wit, as the little convertible pulled away with a squeal of its tyres. 'You'll be taking Miss Nightingale with you this time: East of Eden, could be, somewhere out of this world . . .'

From me to you

Here are six little farewell presents for you, dear reader, the essence of these 99 Ways:

1　Exercise regularly
2　Keep off the cigarettes
3　Think about what you eat, drink and breathe
4　Find fulfilment in work
5　Don't worry – relax
6　Make the most of personal relationships.

THE YEARS OF LIFE QUOTIENT QUIZ

Results you can see in six weeks

It's well enough reading health books, watching health programmes on TV and worrying about your health. You must *do* something if you want to increase your YLL – Years of Life to Live.

Here is a way to improve your YLL quotient. Measure it today and see it grow in weeks. For instance, if you're a sedentary person and start up regular exercise, you get an extra YLL point credited to you immediately. What's more, you can check the benefit: three or four stiff walk-sessions a week will begin to bring your pulse rate down to healthier levels.

Years of Life Quotient

Answer this quiz by scoring one point for each box ticked yes. Be honest! The total is your YLL score. Then pick out your weak items and go through the 99 Ways once again to work away at them. After six weeks, fill in the quiz a second time and see how your YLL total has improved. You should expect extra happy years to come.

YES	NO	
☐	☐	1. Do you exercise regularly?
☐	☐	2. Do you have the recommended health checks for your sex and age?
☐	☐	3. Is fresh fruit and veg part of your daily diet?
☐	☐	4. Are you a non-smoker?
☐	☐	5. Do you have a satisfactory sex life?
☐	☐	6. Is your weight reasonable?
☐	☐	7. Do you sleep well?
☐	☐	8. Do you get enjoyment from job or daily activity?
☐	☐	9. Have you a pastime, hobby or outside interest?
☐	☐	10. Have you enough close friends?
☐	☐	11. Is your alcohol intake moderate?
☐	☐	12. Are you strictly off dangerous drugs?
☐	☐	13. Are you moderate with legal drugs?
☐	☐	14. Are you able to relax?
☐	☐	15. Can you deal effectively with stress?
☐	☐	16. Is your animal-fat consumption moderate?
☐	☐	17. Exercise (again) – is what you do sufficiently aerobic?

Assessment

If you score 17, keep on going until you pass 100!

If you're in the range 11–16, your life-style is well adapted to a good, long life. Keep working at it.

If you're in the range 8–10, you have the chance to do a good deal better. Campaign on one of your zeros at a time.

If you're in the 5–8 range, much work is needed. You can improve immeasurably.

If you're in the 0–4 range, tsk, tsk! Hard, practical application is needed. Perhaps you should start with a talk to your GP.

The 99 Ways